Lessons from the Well

A Devotional for the Divorced and Relationship Impaired

Carol Renee Gitthens

LESSONS FROM THE WELL
A Devotional for the Divorced and Relationship Impaired
2025 © by Carol Renee Gitthens
All rights reserved. Published 2025.

BIBLE SCRIPTURES

Published in the United States of America by

 **SPIRIT MEDIA**

Spirit Media Inc
https://spiritmedia.us

Spirit Media and our logos are trademarks of
Spirit Media Inc
8045 Arco Corporate Drive STE 130
Raleigh, NC 27617
1 (888) 800-3744

Religion & Spirituality > Christian Living > Spiritual Growth

Paperback ISBN: 979-8-89307-175-7
eBook ISBN: 979-8-89307-162-7
PDF ISBN: 979-8-89307-163-4
Library of Congress Control Number: 2025912064

DEDICATION

In April 2023, I was by my father's side night and day. He was in a nursing home on hospice care with many internal complications as a result of Parkinson's Disease. After many days in the Intensive Care Unit, he had returned to the nursing home with about a week to live.

Just a few days before his passing, I experienced one final, meaningful exchange with him. He was resting on his side, and he was looking in the direction of the window. His breathing was slow and labored. I sat in a chair, on the side of his bed, facing him, and his eyes shifted from the window to me. He wanted to speak. I was quiet, patiently waiting to hear his voice once more, any sound at all – a whisper, a single word. All he could give me was his attention and the slightest expressions coming from his beautiful aged eyes, but they transcended the spoken word. I could see love in his pale, feeble countenance. There was sadness that we would be separated, if only for a time. I could see regret for all the things he wished he had done differently. There was so much guilt he held onto. He did his best in recent years to make it right. How I wished I had experienced these tender moments with him as a girl, but I was deeply grateful for them now.

Then, I spoke. I gently took his hand, and after telling him how much I loved him, I tearfully promised him two things...

First, I promised my dad that I would carry the torch of his ministry. I would share the gospel of salvation with the lost. I would speak the truth in love. I would challenge believers to a life of holiness. This is what he did, and it is what he loved. It was a connection we always had with one another, a love and passion for the Word of God, and for the truth.

Second, I promised him I would finish my book. He knew I had been working on this project for several years. He had always recognized this ability in me, and often encouraged me to write.

After I made my promises to him, he gave me the only response his frail and dying body could offer...the slightest nod, and a glimmer in his eyes. Through his hollowed appearance, I could see he was proud of me.

He passed away the night of April 21, 2023. To date, it is the most difficult loss I've experienced.

More than a year after his death, I had finished the book's content. While looking for some of his sermon notes to pass down to one of my sons, I found his Bible among the belongings given to me. His Bible had seen better days, and it showed all the signs of wear from decades of reading and study. I shuffled through it to look at his markings and notes in the margins, and I found a letter I had written to him for Father's Day more than 20 years prior, folded and placed in the middle of its pages. I opened the letter...

> *Dear Dad,*
> *I know I don't call or come around as often as I should, but I think of you often. It is easy to appreciate my childhood as I read the news and see all the terrible things happening in the world. I tell my kids often how thankful we should be. Because of you, I know God in a personal way. Because of you, I am knowledgeable of his Word and his will. Because of you, I was protected and never experienced abuse or the kind of pain so many children have to grow up with. I am grateful I had a dad that could answer my questions about God with the truth of Scripture. I am grateful to have been taught respect and good behavior. I may not have always been good. Let's be honest, I've made some terrible mistakes. But your unconditional love for me is an example of who God is, and it's what has kept me pressing on and never giving up. I hope you have a great day! Thank you for everything!*
>
> *Love,*
> *Renee "Bird"*

I wrote the letter at a time when healing and reconciliation had finally happened between us following my first divorce. Perhaps keeping it in the pages of his Bible was a reminder of all that he did right, when feelings of doubt set in.

The "terrible mistakes" mentioned in my letter are what this book is about. It was through my divorces and, as a result, the ups and downs of our father-daughter relationship, that we both came to a fuller understanding of the grace of God.

The writing process has been deeply emotional for me. Directly or indirectly, everything about it makes me think of my dad. I have often stopped writing to work through the emotions I feel over his absence, because I can't see him every Sunday, because I can't hear his laughter, share my accomplishments, or be on the receiving end of one of his practical jokes. Still, he is forever in my heart.

This book is dedicated to my father, Bishop and Pastor, Ronald Keith Gitthens, and to his cherished memory.

FOREWORD

I have had the wonderful privilege of meeting and getting to know Renee Gitthens. She is a woman of integrity with a spirit that exudes the love of Chr st. This journal is not a book that praises or justifies one of the most controversial and divisive topics within the church; instead, it points to the healing power of Jesus, despite our choices in life. Renee has experienced the sovereign grace of God and now sits on the other side of pain, loss, and despair. She reminds us that we are lost without our first love, and losing our focus on Him will always lead to loss, hopelessness, and desperation. I pray this message finds you on a desperate Damascus Road that leads you back to your first love, Jesus.

Stephanie Hensley

Author, "When the Lilacs Bloom"

Contents

CHAPTER ONE
A Place Once Known as Virtue..7

CHAPTER TWO
The Struggle Didn't Start with Divorce 13

CHAPTER THREE
From Pie in the Sky to Fly in the Soup 26

CHAPTER FOUR
Who Told You That You Were Naked? 40

CHAPTER FIVE
Lessons from the Well 51

CHAPTER SIX
A Closer Look 75

CHAPTER SEVEN
Victim or Victor: Steps to Overcoming 96

CHAPTER EIGHT
To Judge, or not to Judge, that is the Question............................104

CHAPTER NINE
Moving Forward 112

CHAPTER ONE:

A Place Once Known as Virtue

An Allegory of First Love and Loss of Innocence

Virtue was mine. It was a landscape adorned with the beauty of innocence, unspoiled, and blooming with endless possibilities. Nothing was dead or brittle. Every plant flourished in youthful anticipation, and every fruit and flower thrived with hope. The meadow was clothed with wild flowers of many vibrant colors, descending gracefully to the clear, babbling stream. Near the stream was a well encircled with large stones, and the water from it was as clean and pure as a young girl's heart. Virtue was a sanctuary; the well was my heart. It was an expression of all I had imagined love would be, and it was thriving with the deep affection I felt for one young man.

Each day, I walked to the well to draw water, and now, he walked with me. We spent our days together, barefoot and carefree. His presence was the peace I felt beneath the shade of the trees. My love for him was the expanse of the baby blue sky. His arms were the warm embrace of the sun. And when he said, "I love you," the sound of his voice was a cool breeze swirling gently through a million oak leaves, dancing softly on their branches.

But with all the love I had shown him, he slowly grew distant. More often, I walked to the well alone. At times, I would find him at the bluff, his eyes fixed on the horizon. His heart seemed a thousand miles from me. I tried to rationalize his indifference, but deep inside I feared he might leave me there alone.

He took me by the hand one day and led me to the midst of the sanctuary, to a place we had never been. It was hedged about, and securely gated. Purity was the lock, and Promise was the key. Beyond the gateway was all I had to give him. There was nothing left, nothing else I could offer. My conscience grew uneasy, but I gave him the key.

I was challenged within my spirit as he unlocked the gate. I hoped it would cause his restless heart to settle and he would remain with me. We walked into the garden, hand in hand, but regret brought a foreboding sky. It quickly grew dark, and the clouds began to stir. A fierce wind blew with increasing strength as I wrestled in my spirit with what I had done. Leaves and branches were strewn about, and one guilty thought at a time, the land was left in complete disarray.

My spirit was just as scattered. I was fearful and ashamed. I believed his presence in my world would overcome the guilt that stormed within me. I rationalized my actions in one moment, and was afraid of the consequences in the next. Still, I held tight to him. And it seemed now, for the sake of my conscience ... I had to.

And what was I to do with the mess we had created? I couldn't show regret; I couldn't change my mind. He would leave, I would be left to pick up the pieces alone, and Virtue would remain a ramshackle. No, we should marry now. We must. I continued with feigned content, desiring to be close to him as my spirit warred with my flesh. When we were apart, I worked tirelessly to gather debris and hide fallen limbs, but no amount of work would restore the beauty of what I had lost.

He had my whole heart; he had all of me. Still, he returned to that place of indifference. Each time I would find him at the bluff, looking toward the skyline, I could feel the distance growing between us. I knew our time together was coming to an end. I was betrayed and rejected. My spirit was anxious with uncertainty. He said he loved me. I wanted to believe him, but I could see the heart-rending truth in his eyes. I could feel it in his words ... it wasn't the same. I knew in the deepest recesses of my heart that I would soon face the ultimate hurt.

One day, I walked to the bluff to see him, but he was not there. My heart raced with worry! I quickly ran to the meadow, and then to the well, but I could not find him. For many hours, I searched and searched all of Virtue – and when my body was tired and worn, I returned to the bluff and waited for him until the sun had faded to a warm glow. I prayed he would return, but deep in my spirit I knew he was not coming back. The storms began once again, a fierce rain came, and it carried on through the night. I cried many tears. Days, weeks, and months went by, but there was no sight of him.

It was a heartbreak which changed the trajectory of my life for years to come. It wasn't simply the loss of my first love. It was the culmination of events and circumstances which secured my belief that I was unworthy of anything better than what I had lost, in spite of the idyllic life I had imagined. Virtue was gone for good, and I would never be able to return it to its former glory.

So, with passing time, the flowers wilted and the branches of the trees grew brittle. The sky was clouded over. I felt pain to my very core. I resolved that I would never love that way again, and I would never again allow myself to feel that kind of rejection.

Thirty years, three marriages, and five kids later...

Men have come and gone. Some were "good" by human definition, some had questionable reputations. A few caused great damage. With each failed attempt to love and be loved, Virtue now bore the wounds and scars of many relationship failures in its rugged, dry terrain.

I failed myself, my father, and most importantly, God. This is not what anyone had expected of me, and yet here I was – downcast with guilt and shame, drowning in bad decisions, seemingly unable to stop the ever-increasing degradaticn of a place that was meant to shine with beauty, a place that was intended to be loved and respected by one God-fearing man, forever.

At the gate entrance, I staked a sign with a new name, Vulnerable, population: one. By then, I had found a weakness in myself, something that would for many years cause this land to remain void of beauty and genuine love. I longed for someone to understand my value, and I fell continually to the empty promises of disingenuous men.

Standing despairingly at the bluff, I assessed the desolate view. It had become a place of fierce battles against an onerous foe. I fought a long and ill-fated war. I wielded my sword against every intruder who attempted to infiltrate my defenses and take captive my heart. So, I encapsulated the well with thick, impenetrable walls, built up with stones of fear and distrust. It was dutifully guarded, day and night. The stream was shallow, and the well had become stagnant with self-doubt and insecurity. The cracked earth bore the evidence of relationship casualties. And it was full of them ... husbands, fiancés, and men I never intended to marry.

REFLECTIONS

The allegory symbolizes the mess that can become of our lives even when our motives are sincere and borne out of genuine love. It doesn't matter how it began, whether we were foolish and rebellious, or whether we were doing our level best to be wise in our decisions; we live in a world where pain and hurt will find both the reckless and the well-intentioned.

Discuss or Journal

Romantically, when was the first time you said "I love you" to someone? In what ways can you identify with the allegory as it relates to your first relationship experience?

_____

_____

_____

_____

How did the breakup or divorce affect you? How did it change your outlook on love, or your sense of self-worth?

_____

_____

_____

_____

After the breakup or divorce, how did you view the relationship(s) that followed? Did your standards or expectations change?

_____

_____

_____

_____

_____

If yes, in what ways did your standards/expectations change?

_____

_____

_____

_____

Have you ever been in a relationship or marriage you knew was outside of God's will, but you pursued it, anyway? How did it turn out?

_____

_____

_____

_____

How have the adversities you have faced in your relationships affected your relationship with God?

_____

_____

_____

_____

Psalm 71:20 (NKJV) says, "You, who have shown me great and severe troubles, Shall revive me again, And bring me up again from the depths of the earth."

Sometimes our troubles are created by choices we make for ourselves, but God's Word says, "from the depths of the earth you will again bring me up" (Psalm 71:20 NKJV). Restoration is God's nature, and it is his desire. If there is anything I want you to understand from the onset of this book, it is that GOD IS THE RESTORER, and he will again "bring you up," no matter how far you have strayed and no matter how big the mess has become.

A garden left unattended (that is, living apart from God's will) can be quickly overtaken with the weeds of sin and bad decisions. Even so, with work and the right tools it can be brought to new life and beauty.

Make this your anthem of praise and hope each day you awake, and set your thoughts accordingly... GOD WILL RESTORE.

GOD will restore.

"He heals the brokenhearted and binds up their wounds. He counts the number of the stars; He calls them by name. Great is our Lord, and mighty in power." - Psalm 147:3-5 (NKJV)

God WILL restore.

"Therefore I say to you, whatever you ask for in prayer, believe that you have received it, and it will be yours." This, of course, is whatever is in accordance with his will. You can be sure that restoration is always his will." - Mark 11:24 (NKJV)

God will RESTORE.

"Bless the Lord, O my soul; And all that is within me, bless his holy name! Bless the Lord, O my soul, and forget not all His benefits: Who forgives all your iniquities, who heals all your diseases, Who redeems your life from destruction, Who crowns you with loving kindness and tender mercies, Who satisfies your mouth with good things, so that your youth is renewed like the eagle's." - Psalm 103:1-5 (NKJV)

He is the Living Water, as we will learn in the story of His interaction with the woman at the well. Life requires water, and God brings redemption when we look to him for living, healing, restorative water. No matter how far we have fallen, no matter how ugly our world has become, God is able to restore our lives and give us a new beginning, something more beautiful than we thought possible.

Prayer: *Heavenly Father, thank you for your heart of restoration and redemption. As I move forward, please give me wisdom to know your will for me and to respond in obedience. Help me to understand the truth of your Word so that I do not become a hindrance, but a help to myself in the healing process. In Jesus' name, Amen.*

CHAPTER TWO:

The Struggle Didn't Start with Divorce

Genesis 25, 26, 27, Genesis 32:24-31, 2 Corinthians 12:9, Isaiah 41:10

My dad called me "Bird". It was special because it was his name for me; no one else called me Bird. With all of the bondage and fear I would experience in the years ahead, *Bird* would become a beautiful expression of the resilient spirit within me, and a symbol of my freedom. I would finally understand it many years later and, with Jesus' help, He would finally set me to flight.

I was raised in a Christian home. My father was a pastor; so we were always at church, either in a service or preparing for services. I grew up with a fair amount of naivety; I was sheltered and mostly unaware of the evil in the world around me.

By any human standard, from the outside looking in, I had everything going for me. I was a healthy, attractive girl. God had blessed me with a good mind and a number of artistic and musical abilities. I knew I was loved. I had every reason to be grateful for my life, and in spite of the dysfunction within our family, I was truly thankful for what I had.

I never questioned the fact that I had three sets of grandparents. I didn't know there was anything unusual about it. No one ever discussed it. That is, until one particular summer my sister, Sarah, and I had gone to visit relatives 400 miles away. It was during our visit that we learned about our mother and that she had died as a result of cancer. Grandma showed us pictures and told us all about the beautiful and gifted person our mother was. She passed away at age 21. I was 17 months old, and my sister was a newborn at the time of her death.

I didn't really know what to do with this new information. I pondered it over the years and slowly realized what I had missed out on. I wondered how different my life would have been if I had had my mother. How I longed to feel that bond with her, to have experienced and remembered it, because it was something I did not have with my dad or my stepmother. Sure, there were special experiences, fun times, and moments we felt connected, but I lived a childhood completely void of affection at home. I could not walk up to my dad and give him a hug. My stepmom was emotionally cold toward me. Keeping a physical distance was something I accepted as normal. I loved my family, but as I grew older, I could see there was a divide in our home.

The relationship I had with my stepmom was hostile at times. I felt no bond or emotional connection to her. She never extended herself to me that way. Jealousy was a very real issue with her, and as I grew older, she did not like attention or favor I received from anyone. Living with her became increasingly difficult in my teenage years. To be honest, there were a handful of times I wished my parents would separate. Mom could be so contentious, even violent at times. I often felt out of place. I had a mother who was angry and divisive, and I had a father who loved me very much, but showed me no affection or special attention. When I tried to talk to him about what Mom was doing to me, his response was something like "just try to make the best of it." He never berated her, to me or to anyone else. Even so, I felt appreciation toward her, and I always loved her as the only mother I knew.

My dad was a great role model in many ways. He never participated in activities that were unbecoming of a Christian, much less a pastor. I never heard a cuss word exit his mouth. He never called me a name. Even as a girl, there were many times we would sit in the living room and have biblical discussions, just the two of us, and I would ask him questions about subjects like Dispensationalism and Eschatology. I cherished those times because they were the only conversations with him that delved deeper than the day's itinerary or the "C" on my grade card. No, he was not affectionate. But he would say to me, "Bird, come help your mom set the table," or "C'mon, Bird, let's go to piano lessons." Bird was a hug. It was an "I love you," or "you are special."

I can remember taking mental notes about what kind of wife I would be one day ... Basically, what *not* to do based on my stepmom's behavior. I was never going to nag, I was not going to be controlling, I would be kind to my husband, and I wanted my children to love each other and get along. Like the allegory in *Chapter One,* I daydreamed about the way my life would be, the kind of respect my husband would show me, the kind of wife I would be to him in return, and how much we would cherish our children, the product of our love and affection for one another.

I thought I had it all figured out. I knew what had gone wrong in my childhood, and I was going to make the adjustments necessary for my own family, as a wife and mother. After my second divorce, I still could not see I was a part of the problem, simply because I had no behaviors that were overtly or blatantly destructive, like anger or violence. I had taken all the steps necessary to *not* be like my stepmother. It took many years and countless mistakes to recognize I had issues of my own to work through. Yes, I was hard-working and responsible. I was affectionate and nurturing. I was non-confrontational and did my best to maintain peace. However, within my marriages, I was attempting to develop a connection from a childhood that had been marked with what my body and mind perceived as maternal abandonment.

Sometimes I looked for faults in my spouse that kept me at an emotional distance. I wanted to experience a healthy marital relationship, but I didn't really know what that looked like. I brought into my marriages the repercussions of negative childhood experiences—fear, rejection, and physical abuse. I didn't understand how my early years had affected my ability to trust and attach until I was in my third marriage.

It was the story of Jacob that changed the way I saw God. It was Jacob's heart, in spite of his shortcomings, that taught me how the grace of God works to redeem us in spite of our flaws, in spite of our past, our upbringing, and the utter dysfunction that surrounds us ... even if we are responsible for our own mess! We can do nothing without God, and even as we are in distress over our problems, he is already ahead of us, working it out for our benefit. God showed me through Jacob's story that he is the one who does the accomplishing. God loved and blessed Jacob because he was tenacious about attaining those things which held greater value. Jacob wanted everything God had to offer, and he *strove* for it. This was demonstrated in what he actually *did*, even if it was tainted with human error. Never think you cannot overcome your past, or your upbringing. Never think you have messed up so much that God cannot use your failures, turn them around for your good, and bless you anyway. Keep striving! The struggle was real for Jacob, too

The story begins in Genesis 25:20 when Isaac married Rebekah. Rebekah was unable to conceive, so Isaac pleaded with the Lord on her behalf. The Lord granted Isaac's request and Rebekah became pregnant with twins, but family dysfunction began as early as pregnancy! Rebekah asked God why there was such a battle going on within her womb. God told her that in her womb were two nations, two peoples would be separated from her body, and one people shall be stronger than the other people. The elder shall serve the younger.

She gave birth to twin sons, Esau and Jacob. Esau was the first to be born, coming from her womb red in appearance, and hairy. Jacob followed, but had his hand around Esau's heel, which was another indication of the battle between the boys that had been going on within her womb.

Esau grew to become a skilled hunter, while Jacob was a pastoralist, tending to the livestock. Esau was his father's favorite; Isaac admired Esau for his hunting skills and the delicious meals he would provide for the family. Jacob, however, was favored by his mother. I'm certain Jacob knew his father was partial to Esau; and Esau likely understood the same of his mother. I wonder how this made each of them feel. This likely created some competition between the brothers, even before the real trouble began.

The Birthright and the Blessing were two very important rites, or customs, in those days. Esau had a lot to look forward to, and it should have motivated him to take care of and protect what was rightfully his. Esau had the birthright, an honor bestowed only upon the firstborn son, in this case, even by just minutes. However, the Blessing was a kind of last will and testament, and could be given to anyone in the family the father chose. A greater blessing could be given if that child also held the birthright. Because Esau was Isaac's favorite, he was also set to receive the Blessing from his father.

But as the "supplanter," Jacob had devious plans. Genesis 25:29-34 tells us that Jacob cooked up a delicious stew while his brother, Esau, was away hunting. Esau came in from the field very tired and weak. Esau asked Jacob for some of his stew, but Jacob replied, "Sell me your birthright as of this day." Esau's response was, essentially, "Look, I'm about to die. What good is the birthright to me anyway, if I am dead?" Jacob asked him to swear again, so Esau swore to him and sold his birthright to Jacob. Jacob gave Esau bread and stew of lentils. Esau ate and drank, and then went his way. Then the last sentence of verse 34 (NKJV) says, *"Thus Esau despised his birthright."*

The word "despised" does not mean that he hated his birthright or that he had strong, negative feelings toward it. Rather, Esau considered it of little importance; he was indifferent. The birthright would have given Esau a greater inheritance than his brother. It would have established him as a leader in his family, both physically and spiritually. Perhaps that is why Esau despised it, and why he could not obtain the favor of God. There was more to it than the receiving of wealth and possessions. As a leader, service and obedience to God were also expected, and this was not something Esau cared about.

Think about the parallels here, as it pertains to relationships. We see that Jacob, in spite of all his shortcomings, knew what had value and he pursued those things. He *tried*. He did something. We will also see in the story that this only brought him closer to God. God loved Jacob for this in spite of his sin and devious ways. He strove, he battled, and he struggled because he valued what, ultimately, could only be given by God. Esau did not hold the same values, and he sold his birthright to Jacob for a cup of soup! Esau's situation became uncomfortable, and it was too difficult for him. As a result, he gave up something of great worth and gained the disfavor of God.

Genesis chapter 27 begins with Isaac, the father, being bed bound, blinded, and near death. The time had come for Isaac to bestow the Blessing to Esau. He called Esau to his bedside and asked him to take his weapons and go out to the field and hunt game, and make him some savory food, the kind that Isaac loved, and he would give Esau the blessing when this was done. So, Esau did as his father asked of him, and he went to the field to hunt game.

Rebekah overheard it and came up with a plan. She instructed Jacob to bring her two of the best kids of the goats. She would make Isaac the savory food he desired, and Jacob would present it to his blind father as if he were Esau. Jacob dressed in Esau's clothing so that he smelled like the field. The skin of the goats was used to cover Jacob's hands and a part of his neck, so that Isaac would believe Jacob was his hairy son, Esau.

Jacob presented Isaac with the stew, and Isaac, believing Jacob was Esau, gave Jacob a hefty blessing.

Genesis 27:27-29

"Surely, the smell of my son is like the smell of a field which the Lord has blessed.

Therefore, may God give you of the dew of heaven, of the fatness of the earth, and plenty of grain and wine.

Let peoples serve you, and nations bow down to you, be master over your brethren, and let your mother's sons bow down to you.

Cursed be everyone who curses you, and blessed be those who bless you!"

When Esau returned from the field and made his stew, he presented it to his father. Isaac realized what he had done, and that he had been tricked. Isaac said, "Who? Where is the one who hunted game and brought it to me? I ate all of it before you came, and I have blessed [Jacob] – and indeed he shall be blessed." - Genesis 27:33 (NKJV)

Esau cried bitterly, and asked Isaac to bless him also, but Isaac said, "Your brother came with deceit and has taken away your blessing."

And Esau said, "Is he not rightly named Jacob? For he has supplanted me these two times. He took away my birthright, and now look, he has taken away my blessing!" - Genesis 27:36 (NKJV)

Isaac told Esau that he had made Jacob his master, but he gave him an inferior blessing:

Then Isaac his father answered and said to him: "Behold, your dwelling shall be of the fatness of the earth, and of the dew of heaven from above, by your sword you shall live, and you shall serve your brother, and it shall come to pass, when you become restless, that you shall break his yoke from your neck." - Genesis 27:39, 40 (NKJV)

Esau hated his brother, Jacob. He decided he would remain at his father's side until his passing, then he would find Jacob and kill him. Rebekah knew this, and she warned Jacob, instructing him to travel to where his uncle, Laban, lived and to remain there until Esau had time to cool off. Jacob didn't stop his deceitful practices when he went to stay with Laban. He continued to deceive and take advantage of people.

There are a few things about this story that impressed me as I thought both about my childhood and what I had tried to overcome as a mother in my relationship with my own husband and children.

First, this was a family with the typical dysfunctionality of any other home. It was a family divided down the middle. Can you imagine a mother favoring one of her sons so much that she actually conspires against her other son? And these four were not even a blended family! Isaac wasn't even trying to be fair. The birthright rightfully belonged to Esau, but he could have given the Blessing to anyone. Still he chose to give Esau everything, intending to leave out his other son, Jacob, completely.

Maybe this favoritism from Isaac to Esau is why Rebekah favored Jacob, who might have been unappreciated for the work he did, and his role in the family. Rebekah also knew what the Lord had said, that "the elder shall serve the younger"- Genesis 25:23 (NKJV). I can think of a number of families who have a son or daughter whose work or overall success outshines the other siblings, or one child who feels he or she can never do enough to receive the same praise as their brother or sister. Maybe Rebekah witnessed this partiality from Isaac to Esau from the time the twins were young and, as a mother, it made her compassionate toward Jacob.

The Blessing that was intended for Esau did not have to include Jacob bowing to and serving Esau, but it did. Perhaps it was used by Isaac to rectify the birthright debacle. Isaac could have simply blessed his son with health and abundance, and maybe even dominion over peoples outside their family, but his blessing did much more than that by making Jacob incapable of ever rising above Esau or being anything more than in a position of subservience to him. And if that wasn't enough, the Blessing ends with *"Cursed be everyone who curses you, and blessed be those who bless you!"* - Genesis 27:29 (NKJV). So, Jacob would have been powerless to do anything but bless Esau, even in Esau's hatred for Jacob for cheating him out of his birthright. That is, if things had gone as Isaac had planned.

But God had already spoken. The elder shall serve the younger. It is what God says it is, and it will be what God says it will be. Man cannot thwart God's plans. If you are a child of God, there is not a person or a force on this earth that can keep you from God's purpose for you (read Isaiah 54:17). Both Esau and Jacob were sinners. Each had their own personal inner battles. But Esau was not spiritually minded. He did not care, and therefore he deserved neither the birthright nor the Blessing.

Likewise, God's providence in your situation is not based on your good works, on your ability to behave to sinless perfection, or to make the kind of decisions the church world thinks you should be making in the timeframe you should be making them. Rather, it is based on faith; it is rooted in something more, something greater. That is all God needs to advance you. As with Jacob, it is a journey which begins with a mustard seed of faith and a desire for what can only come from God. With that kind of determination, real change will happen in due season.

Even with all of Jacob's striving, beginning with grabbing the heel of Esau from within the womb, his efforts would have been futile without God. Jacob might have been born last, but God had already determined his place. Despite his deceptive practices and trickery, he would move forward to pursue God with his whole heart, and would eventually step into his calling. He might have felt inferior all those years prior to gaining the Blessing, but God knows what he's doing, and he foreknew Jacob's every move.

Never let your current circumstances decide your outcome, and don't allow your past to push its way into your plans. Lay hold of your blessing! It will require altering your decision-making processes to something that demonstrates to God that you want what he has for you. You cannot be focused on instant gratification and temporary pleasures, as Esau was, then expect God to do great things in your life. You must be spiritually minded; you must desire to have the mind of Christ. Be a Jacob, chase after the blessings of God, and see how he will work in your life in spite of your failures and shortcomings.

When we look at this family, we can draw a reasonable conclusion that, even in the bloodline of Jesus, there were complicated familial relationships. It is simply a product of the human condition. We may believe our circumstances are unique or more challenging, but every family that appears to be perfect actually has its own struggles, some more serious than you could ever imagine. It's simply unavoidable, and the perfect family is a fairytale.

Jacob's problems didn't end there. He left one dysfunctional family, running from a brother who wanted him dead, to another dysfunctional family with an uncle who was also angry with him. Jacob had married Laban's daughters, Leah and Rachel. After he had worked for Laban a total of twenty years, he left secretly with his wives, family, and most of the livestock (a result of another clever stunt). He knew Laban was angry over the livestock situation. God spoke to Jacob and told him to return to the land of his fathers. On the third day of their journey, Laban learned of their departure, and Laban and his brothers hotly pursued Jacob for seven days. In Genesis 31:24, through a dream given to Laban, God ultimately prevented him from doing any harm to Jacob. So, when Laban and his brothers found Jacob, a covenant was made.

After running from and then settling the matter with Laban, Jacob was warned by his messengers that now Esau was coming for him, and with 400 men. Of course, this made Jacob very distressed! After dividing his family and livestock and sending them in two different directions, he camped there, waiting for Esau with a gift of livestock, hoping it would cool Esau's anger. And Jacob prayed. He feared for his life, and for the safety of his family. At the bottom of the proverbial pit he had dug for himself, Jacob reminded God of his promise.

Do you think Jacob felt entitled to God's protection as he recounted his sin and all he had done to gain what he had acquired? I don't think so. Jacob knew his constant deception and trickery were the reasons he was now in a place of fear and desperation. He knew he was fully responsible for what was about to happen. And yet he called on God.

In Genesis 32:12 (NKJV), talking to God, Jacob says, *"For You said, 'I will surely treat you well, and make your descendants as the sand of the sea, which cannot be numbered for multitude.'"*

Since Jacob was in fear of his life and the lives of his family, it seems logical that he would entreat the Lord in this way. After all, God *did* promise Jacob he would treat him well ... and his promise to make the number of Jacob's descendants as the sand of the sea would necessitate that Jacob and his family come out of this ordeal alive.

There have been many times I have prayed in this manner when I am afraid, by reminding God of his promises, even as my circumstances are spinning out of control. As I pray, I am reassured that what God has spoken, I must believe, even when I am experiencing great anxiety over a seemingly hopeless situation. If God says in his Word I am an overcomer, then that's what I am. If he says he is working all things out for my good, then that is what is happening, even in the face of trials and tribulation. If God says his love casts out fear, then why should I be anxious over anything? And if he says his grace is sufficient, why would I worry about my insufficiency?

That night, Jacob encountered God. Genesis 32:24-31 (NKJV) says, *"Then Jacob was left alone; and a Man wrestled with him until the breaking of day. Now when He (the Man) saw that He did not prevail against Jacob, He touched the socket of his hip; and the socket of Jacob's hip was out of joint as He wrestled with him. And He said, 'Let Me go, for the day breaks.' But Jacob said, 'I will not let You go unless You bless me.' So, He said to him, 'What is your name?' He said, 'Jacob.' And He said, 'Your name shall no longer be called Jacob, but Israel; for you have struggled with God and with men, and have prevailed.' Then Jacob asked, saying, 'Tell me Your name, I pray.' And He said, 'Why is it that you ask about My name?' and He blessed him there. So, Jacob called the name of the place Penuel: 'For I have seen God face to face, and my life is preserved.' Just as he crossed over Penuel the sun rose on him, and he limped on his hip."*

Jacob wanted yet another blessing! His life was not only preserved, but he was blessed and given a new name, *Israel*. He was struck in the hip and limped for the rest of his life, I believe, as a reminder that his sufficiency rests in God alone, not in his own abilities.

"And He has said to me, 'My grace is sufficient for you, for My strength is made perfect in weakness.' Most gladly, therefore, I will rather boast about my weaknesses, so that the power of Christ may dwell in me." - 2 Corinthians 12:9 (NKJV)

Have you ever wrestled with God? In my marital conflicts, in times I was afraid or deeply hurting, I would pace around my house, from one room to another, praying with a raised voice, "God! Are you going to continue to allow this!? Yes, I trust you, but I am afraid!! How long must this go on? I cannot endure this any longer ... please, do something!" There were even times I retreated to the floor in my closet, with the door shut, crying and begging God to bring an end to my suffering and restore peace. I was desperate! I felt anguish in those moments, and I cried from the deepest part of my spirit, pleading with God to change the situation.

Can you relate? Did you ever get tired of running, tired of fighting, sick of being afraid, so desperate to find peace that you cried out to God to plead for help, or to question his "absence?" I imagine Jacob also felt continually threatened and afraid. Maybe he believed he was going to die by his brother's hand. Because Esau had 400 men with him, perhaps Jacob feared he would lose everything in a nasty battle. He had already dealt with Laban, and now Esau seemed to be a threat that simply wouldn't go away. He was tired of running, tired of fighting it, sick of looking over his shoulder – and everything came to a head that night. He pleaded for yet another blessing. He wanted assurance, and he was once again fighting for it. At his birth, he was grabbing at the heel of Esau – and now he was grabbing at the heel of God.

"Do not leave until you bless me!" - Genesis 32:26 (NKJV)

And God, indeed, blessed him. Through tribulation, God brought Jacob to a place where he could no longer rely on himself and his tricks and deception. It was through Jacob's trials that a genuine relationship with God was established.

In this culture, we desire comfort, convenience, and anything that is easy or pain-free. Of course, we want a peaceful life. Many strive for an idyllic existence that elicits envy from others. Sometimes we do our best to deny any kind of weakness or failure, and we try to avoid criticisms or to avert trials.

But the story of Jacob gives us a different perspective on the idea of conflict and struggling in our closest relationships, and even in our relationship to God. This was a man who lived through some extremely difficult circumstances, not from outsiders, but from his own flesh and blood. Though his deception was to blame for much of his struggles, there was a lot more to his story. He was not favored by his father, as Esau was. This likely caused feelings of rejection, and perhaps some hostility between the brothers from the very beginning. Jacob felt he had to cheat to get the things he had. He was mistreated and taken advantage of by Laban. He worked 14 years to marry the woman he loved (though he had agreed to seven), and now he was being hunted down by his angry brother and a small army! He was used, mistreated, and hated. Yet Jacob cared enough to continue to strive. He didn't give up, even when he made poor decisions. God was with him for this reason, and he was blessed in spite of his mistakes.

Friends, it takes the hard stuff in our lives to build character. And it is the fight for God's blessing that gets his attention, even if you seem to be doing it all wrong for a while. If God is on our side, trials and tribulation can only strengthen us in the end. We learn forgiveness, patience, self-control, and every good fruit we should be yielding as a child of God. How can we practice genuine love if we are not confronted with hate or indifference? How would we learn to forgive without experiencing the pain of offenses? Can we grow in patience without the presence of conflict?

I am not suggesting that we allow ourselves to be doormats to abusive people. However, when we find ourselves in these painful situations, and we make our way out of them by the grace of God, *how we move forward will depend on our perspective of what is behind us.* Don't be bitter. Don't be resentful. Don't be unforgiving. Learn from it, grow from it, and thank God for helping you out of it. Jacob messed up badly, over and over again. When he could no longer depend on his own craftiness to get him out of his precarious situation, when he was exhausted and at the end of himself, that is the place he truly found a genuine and meaningful relationship with God.

I had to learn in my own situation that everything in my past, good and bad, was a part of my journey. It was my story, my testimony, and the reason I am who I am today. The emotional scars aren't present to remind me of my pain; rather, they remind me of the freedom and strength I have in Jesus Christ. Rejection, fear, and abandonment began as a small child, and those feelings continued throughout my adult years. However, each challenge I have faced has been an opportunity to trust God and to know him in a deeper way. When you have come to the end of yourself, and you have nowhere left to run, God will meet you right where you are. He will give you a new name, as he did Jacob, that being – a new life, new purpose, renewed hope, and a new beginning.

The struggle is real. It is inevitable. You cannot get around it, you cannot make it disappear, and there is no shortcut. But God has promised us that we can endure it.

"Fear not, for I am with you; be not dismayed, for I am your God; I will strengthen you, I will help you, I will uphold you with my righteous right hand." - Isaiah 41:10 (NKJV)

I am so thankful that God is on my side. I'm grateful I can wake in the morning and call out to Him, and he hears me. I choose to trust Him in every trial, and I know He is working it all out for my good (Romans 8:28). The same is true for every brother and sister in Christ Jesus.

REFLECTIONS

Discuss or Journal

What wounds do you carry from childhood (abuse, abandonment, death, etc.)?

_____
_____
_____
_____

Have they negatively impacted your relationships as an adult? If so, how?

_____
_____
_____
_____

Read Proverbs 3:5-6. If we want God to help us, what must we do?

1. _____
_____

2. _____
_____

3. _____
_____

4. _____
_____

On line #3 above, you should have written, "In all your ways, acknowledge God." This is a direct stipulation for what follows, "and he shall direct your paths," or "he will make your paths straight." In other words, if we want God to direct our path, we start by acknowledging Him in *all* our ways. Jacob is a great example of tenacity for the deeper things of God. Esau, however, better represents many professing Believers ... complacent and uncommitted, holding little value to what has been gifted to them. If you value the Word of God, you will study its content. If you desire to please God, you will seek his will in prayer, and a pattern of better behavior will follow. As we grow closer to God, we will mature spiritually. What we couldn't forgive before, we can now show grace. We find value in ourselves and gain confidence, we raise the standard, set appropriate boundaries, love more deeply, serve more sincerely, and see more clearly. All things become new! Isn't that what He promised?

"Therefore, if anyone is in Christ, he is a new creation; old things have passed away; behold, all things have become new." - 2 Corinthians 5:17 (NKJV)

As Christians, we don't pursue the things of God as we ought! I have talked to more Christians giving themselves permission to sin or simply meander in spiritual complacency than I see believers who are as determined as Jacob was, when he had come to the end of himself, to acquire the blessing of God. And we wonder why we are stuck in a cycle!

Focus on what God wants from *you*—in your behavior, your thoughts, your actions, and your words, and let Him worry about everyone else. What is keeping you from a closer walk with God? In what ways will you purpose to make your relationship with God a better one?

_____

_____

_____

_____

_____

_____

_____

_____

_____

_____

_____

_____

_____

_____

Prayer: *Heavenly Father, thank You for Your salvation and the grace You have lavished on me. Lord, I want more of Your presence in my life, and I am asking You to please direct my path. I know by Your Word what changes I need to make in my spirit, in my life, and in my relationships. I will do my best to do Your will, and to be more pleasing to You. I ask You to continue to show grace to me as I show grace to others. I will forgive those who have hurt me, as You have forgiven me. When I am afraid, confused, or angry, I place my trust in You and will continue to do what pleases You. As I follow Your lead, please heal the wounds of my past. When I am struggling, help me to recall Your promises. In Jesus' name, Amen.*

CHAPTER THREE:

From Pie in the Sky to Fly in the Soup

Romans 8, Ephesians 4:31,32, 1 John 2:1-2, Galatians 5:13, John 10:27-30

If I ever feel content in my singleness and relatively lonesome existence, a trip to the grocery store is sure to "remedy" it. On any given Saturday, it's typical to see married couples shopping and taking care of this mundane task together. That kind of companionship is something I rarely experienced in a combined three husbands and 29 years of marriage. I feel especially lonely when I witness a man loving and doting on his wife, obviously quite content to be with her. How I would love to feel a strong hand around my waist and a gentle kiss on my cheek. I am sincerely happy that the couple appears to be successful at this complex thing we call marriage. More satisfying is the positive energy emanating from their young children; it is almost palpable in their light-hearted and genuinely loving exchanges. I'm certain they have experienced their own ups and downs, perhaps even some serious complications, but have come out on the other side seemingly as strong as they were the day they married. "Good for them," I might think of the happy family, "you're doing it right." Deep down, I long for the same kind of cozy connection in the freezer section of the grocery store—or anywhere, for that matter.

As a young woman, I had believed in a 'pie in the sky' kind of love—an unrealistic notion that my husband would never violate my trust, would always be faithful, and never say a hurtful word. Even after reality hit and my expectations took a nosedive into the depths of my insecurities, I often wondered what prevented me from having an ordinary, everyday kind of relationship with a man. Nevermind perfect. Forget about being incredibly happy and madly in love. Why couldn't I have a marriage that was "fairly good, even if unremarkable?"

After my second divorce, I was shopping at a local store, dutifully pushing my cart from aisle to aisle to purchase all the family needs for the week ahead. All was going well, and then it happened.

"Mommy!"

I turned around to look for my child (because that's what we moms do even when our kids aren't with us). I noticed a little boy, his sisters, and his parents browsing in the electronics department. I observed the adorable family in 2 or 3 second increments, trying not to be intrusive on their privacy. I noticed even with all the commotion coming from the boy and his little sister, the husband was focused on his wife who, I might add, was no supermodel. Rather, she had all the characteristics of a typical busy mom with three kids: comfortable clothes, pony tail, and barely-there makeup. He was clearly enjoying his time with her, shopping for a new alarm clock—and he couldn't keep his hands off of her. He was rubbing her shoulders, embracing her from behind, and kissing her on the cheek as she made her selection from the shelf.

There was a feeling of emptiness that washed over me like a tsunami wave on what I thought would be a sunny and relaxing day at the beach. What started out as an uneventful trip to the store had just become a reminder of the wholeness, togetherness, and unconditional love I did not have. All the negative feelings set in. Regret. Anxiety. Confusion. I asked myself the nagging questions that had yet to be answered. Is a healthy relationship possible for me? What redeemable quality does this lovely woman have that I lack? What's more, I have witnessed countless women who are secure in themselves and their relationships, who don't feel like they have to be anything spectacular to receive their husband's love, devotion, and attention. Why couldn't I have that? Do I not deserve it? Why did I feel I had to earn love by my appearance, or to lose myself in a long list of expectations just so I could be "loved" with limits and conditions?

And then there are the tougher questions. Does God require me to stay in my marriage at any cost? Is that what it means to take up our cross and follow Jesus? Or did He really come to deliver us from oppression and to free us from bondage? And if that is true, how might I have experienced that freedom *and* saved my marriage? Is it sin to remarry? If it is sinful, why does the Apostle Paul say, "It is better to marry than to burn with passion?" If God reserves marriage only for those who have not been previously married, then what will become of my walk with God as a single person who may struggle with celibacy?

I did the remainder of my shopping awakened to the absence of a man and his affection. I tried to analyze my situation and I asked myself, "What is wrong with me?" With every failed marriage or relationship that has followed, I had become increasingly cynical about love and commitment, doubting that I will ever have the security of familiar arms embracing me in the Electronics Department—or the freezer section—no matter how I looked, or what we had been through. To experience that kind of tenderness and unconditional devotion is all I ever wanted. This was not the plan, mind you. And I wasn't intentionally careless in my decisions, or rebellious. I had lofty ideas of love and marriage, God-fearing goals. I had every intention of living the dream—one man, one woman, for life.

Let me talk about "*the plan*." For many of us church-bred teenagers, what you imagine your life to be 20 years down the road is a combination of what you know everyone in your religious family expects, and what our stargazing, naive minds dream up. And it goes a little something like this...

You devote yourself to sexual purity as a teenager. That's the way you were raised, so you decide you will honor God by being chaste until you marry. You graduate high school, start college, and meet a really sweet guy in your English class. He asks you out and you begin dating. He is very handsome, and it doesn't hurt that he has great biceps. He is smart, respectful, hardworking, and has a successful career ahead. Soon, he becomes your best friend. He is a Christian; he prays and reads his Bible. Oh yes, and he is crazy about you. He thinks you are the most beautiful girl he has ever set eyes on and he reminds you of it often. He is the culmination of everything on your Husband Wish List; he is everything you ever dreamed of. He has a good family, and he loves your family, too. What's better, you tell him that you are saving sexual intimacy for marriage, and you are relieved to learn he has the same God-fearing goal.

After just weeks of dating, you are sitting in college English class, using a spiral notebook and your favorite pink pen to practice a different signature in your most lovely cursive handwriting. You hope his last name will become yours one day, and you admire the way it looks on paper. You daydream of how beautiful your children will be and you think of baby names, secretly, of course, because you don't want to scare him. Yes, you are in love; you are totally smitten. You can't imagine a future with anyone else.

Months later, it is your birthday, and you suspect the big day has come. You enjoy a romantic dinner by candlelight and later he asks you to take a stroll on the beach. You are hand in hand, and the two of you stop briefly to admire the gorgeous sunset illuminating the sky with shades of orange and deep purple. You look up at him with such admiration. The butterflies have never gone away. He is so wonderful. He gazes at you with a gentle look of love. Realizing that the right moment has come, he lifts a small black box out of his pocket. You look at the box and pretend to be taken by surprise, then look back at him like a deer in headlights. Is he going to...? Will he...? He slowly drops to one knee. "You are everything a man could ever want and need. I love you, and I will love you forever. Will you do me the honor of being my wife?"

"Wow!" you reply, as you cup your hands to your mouth in elated surprise, "Of course I will be your wife! YES!" He nervously slides the ring onto your finger. You embrace each other and share a tender kiss as the last rays of sunlight mellow to a glow behind the sea.

The wedding plans begin. You can hardly contain your excitement as you organize every detail, poring over dozens of bridal magazines for luxurious yet cost-effective ideas. You marry in the shortest possible time your grand wedding plans will allow because neither one of you can handle much more of the wait and anticipation of your first night together.

The big day arrives. The ceremony is held at the same beautiful beach where he proposed. It is a comfortable 73 degrees and there is not a dark cloud in sight. He is overcome with happiness as he watches you saunter gracefully down the sandy aisle. Your beautiful, deservedly-white dress flows softly in the gentle ocean breeze. You are the picture of virgin-bride perfection. The wedding goes as planned; the reception is fun and lively. Having held to your commitment to remain pure, the honeymoon in Jamaica is awkward, but amazing nonetheless.

Two years later, you have the first of several perfect children. Within ten years, you have the standard three kids, proud ownership of a silver 7-passenger minivan, and a white picket fence surrounding a lovely, creamy yellow bungalow. Life is great. A few ups and downs here and there, but for the most part, you know nothing but marital happiness. There is no doubt in your mind that you will one day celebrate a 25th wedding anniversary, then a 40th and a 50th. When you are frail and aged, you will die in each other's arms and share a headstone engraved with a heart and interlocking wedding bands.

Can you identify? With many added details of our romantic imaginations, and a few exaggerations, this is the general idea of the way most of us thought love would be. One man, one woman, in love, for life. We don't marry intending to be divorced one day. We are expecting nothing less than success. And maybe that's a little bit of the problem.

Maybe our unreasonable expectations set us up for failure, believing things have gone far too wrong and marriage is much harder than we expected—when marriage is actually a sacrificial and sometimes difficult demonstration of love, just as Jesus taught us in Matthew 5:43-48. That is, love your enemies and pray for those who persecute you. At times, the "enemy" can be the one we are married to. Sometimes we give up too quickly and we don't understand the selfless actions required in maintaining a healthy relationship with our spouse. In any other relationship, we can simply choose to disassociate ourselves from the person who is causing us hurt or frustration. A marriage, however, is a gift, because the person to which we are spiritually bound forces the issues of our heart to the surface, and genuine love requires that we contend with those areas that need to be sanctified. It necessitates real change within us in order to uphold our vows. Yet as difficult as that may seem, I wish it were that easy for all of us.

With all the hellfire and brimstone messages I've heard over the years about adultery—with every conversation I've listened to at fellowship dinners about Brother and Sister So-and-So and their impending divorce, whose fault it must be, and "what an awful shame"—when I pursue ministry and in the requirements for licensing notice in their understanding of biblically-justified wording that those who have been divorced after salvation have no shot, so don't even bother applying—when my grandpa would say things like "My, my. I would hate to stand before God one day having been divorced."—Yeah. I got the picture. God hates divorce. It is disgraceful and detestable and, in their minds, the first on the list of superbad, oh-no-you-didn't, now-you've-really-gone-and-done-it abominations punishable by God's everlasting wrath. Every word spoken about it in my world was drenched with a feeling of impending doom for the man (or woman) who would dare file for a dissolution from their spouse, even if they were in fear for their safety!

It is no wonder we spend so much time beating ourselves up trying to make things right, only to make another mistake. We don't receive the level of help we need with recovery and healing. Instead, the fact we have been divorced comes back in different ways to bedevil us—from personal guilt, to real-world struggles, to limitations placed on us by judgmental church folk.

It is like the house fly buzzing around the dinner table that eventually finds a landing place on your nose. You try to "shoo" it away. It flies off for a brief moment and then returns to your nose. No matter how much you wave your hand around to try and rid yourself of its pesky persistence, it will not leave you alone. And once it is done pestering you, it dives straight for your bowl of delicious, homemade soup, contaminating it with every tiny, filthy part of its ugly, unwelcome body. It simply wouldn't go away. It wasn't enough that the fly had to disturb your plans, now as it flits about the surface, it has completely changed them.

The aftermath of divorce is much the same. You have come through on the other end of all the legalities, you are sitting at the table, napkin in your lap and spoon in hand, ready to put the past behind you and enjoy the next chapter of life. Nevertheless, the buzzing fly is always there, at different times, in different ways. He wants to make sure you never forget, be it through the heartbreaking comments of your children, the disappointment of your family, or witnessing someone else's attentive husband at the store. And if that isn't enough, the guilt you continue to hold onto has a way of "contaminating" and changing your future.

Here is how it really went...

As a young lady in high school, I knew I should remain pure until I married. This wasn't difficult because I was an introvert and very timid around boys anyway. I always knew when I had a young man's interest, so I did my best to avoid any interaction with him and, thus, any conversations that might lead to dates and physical contact. Many of my former male classmates would tell you I was mostly unapproachable. In my innocence and naivety, my mind could only imagine being kissed in an innocent way, like a dashing young gentleman kisses a glamorous leading lady in a classic black and white movie, but the thought of it materializing caused me a bit of anxiety.

By the time I started college, I had mostly overcome my fear of dating. I was working at a local department store when a young man entered my checkout line. He was very handsome, so I took a quick glance at his left hand. No ring (yes!). He paid for his items with a check. I glanced at his name and struck up a shamelessly-flirty conversation. During our brief conversation, I realized he was the man my Sunday School teacher had been trying to set me up with. As I was writing the necessary information on the check, I brought this to his attention, and we shared an awkward laugh over it. I'm sure I was a few shades of red, but I didn't care because I had two minutes to make an impression (hopefully a good one) before he exited my checkout lane—and life—for good.

He left, but returned a short time later with an item he "forgot" to purchase earlier. He asked me on a date and I gave him my phone number. I was elated! This has *got* to be a great guy, and he must be a Christian because he told me in our short conversation that he attended a local Baptist church.

That weekend, he called me and we went out on our first date. He was everything I was looking for. He was a man of faith, good-looking, hard-working, smart, responsible—and great biceps. We continued to date and my feelings for him developed quickly. I fell in love, in the way 18-year-old girls do. He was the best thing that had ever entered my life. And he said he loved me, too. I shared with him that I was reserving sexual intimacy for marriage, and that I was a virgin. I hoped to hear the same, only to be disappointed and a bit jealous when he informed me he had been intimate with only one girl. And just one time.

Sigh. Okay, fine.

At home, while trying to work through the jealousy and disappointment of his past sexual encounter(s) with what I'd like to believe was just one girl (and one time), I practiced signing what I hoped to be my future last name. The possibility of marriage had eventually become a part of our conversations, so I secretly thought of baby names. ...Okay, I later shared one name idea with him, and he laughed at it. Otherwise, everything was going *pretty much* according to plan.

Several months later, it was my birthday and I suspected the big night had come. As I got ready for our date, I imagined a lovely dinner (forget the candlelight) at a somewhat reputable eating establishment free of health code violations. Maybe he would take me for a walk in the park and propose at the pretty, white gazebo. Wherever we were headed, I was dolled up and ready to go.

He was an hour behind schedule, but said he was late getting home from work. He took me to a local barbecue joint for their Friday night special. After dinner and when the sun had set, he drove the two of us to a remote location on a gravel road to make out. After the windows had fogged up, he turned on the overhead light to make his next move and pulled a small box out of the dusty glove compartment. This is the moment I had been waiting for. Is he going to...? Will he...? He opened the box and asked simply, "Will you marry me?" Of course, I said, "Yes!"

Okay, so it wasn't the romantic sunset proposal on the beach. It wasn't on bended knee at the pretty, white gazebo in the park. It wasn't even on bended knee on that remote gravel road amid the lowing cattle ... we didn't even get out of the car. But it was all good. I loved him, he loved me, and the wedding plans began.

Weeks later, something began to shift. It felt as though I was losing him, and I couldn't imagine why. Like the allegory in the first chapter, he was walking to the bluff. He was distant and didn't seem as interested in spending time with me. He didn't take me out on dates as often. When he did, he was frequently very late. One night he even no-showed. That particular evening, I gazed hopelessly out my bedroom window for hours, until the late summer darkness overtook my view of the isolated gravel road. I desperately wanted to see headlights. I reasoned if he arrived hours late, that's okay, as long as he came. I was already making excuses for him. Maybe something happened at work. Maybe he had a flat tire. But it didn't feel right. I wanted to believe he still loved me, but it felt like I was hanging onto the relationship by a thread. What could be wrong? Even if there was a legitimate reason, I felt if he loved me, he would pick up a phone anywhere, and he would call me to let me know.

He eventually called to apologize, and we rescheduled our date. In my desperation to regain his attention, I made a life-changing decision. After our next dinner date, we drove to the home he had purchased for us to live after we married. It was mostly empty, but we moved a few things in, including a record player. We went inside, he put on a Boston vinyl ...and we did things we should not have done. I believed this is what he wanted, and hoped it would keep him committed to me.

But less than a month later, he broke off the relationship completely. I was deeply wounded by his rejection and I spent many nights crying myself to sleep. Over the next 6 months, the pain slowly subsided, and I began to look at the relationship more clearly and not through the haziness of infatuation. I reasoned God knew our marriage would not work, and he was telling me "no". I wasn't sure how things would change after that. All I knew is that I could never get back the innocence I had lost. I had willfully taken a "left turn" away from God's direction for my life. I justified my decision to give myself to my fiance sexually with the belief that we would be married one day. Afterall, I had a ring on my finger. Because of the choice I made that particular evening, I continued a cycle of sinful behavior in the relationships that followed.

It would take decades for me to fully understand why God has commands for us to follow, that those expectations for me (and you) have good reasons, and I should trust God's Word and not the promises of human beings. I could have said "no" to sexual immorality. Even after my sinful compliance, I could have said, "This is not something we should be doing, and we need to stop." I could have returned to the straight path God had intended for me to follow. Instead, this behavior became more comfortable to me than it should have been. After that night with my first love, my disobedience did not stop. I walked straight through the front door of sexual sin with all of my relationship baggage, I set up house, and I made it my dwelling. I was convicted, but I was broken, and I didn't know how to change. I was torn between my love for God and my need for affection, acceptance, and protection in the arms of a strong and loving man.

I married my first husband three years later. We divorced and there was a second marriage, and then a third.

I can look back and thank God for carrying me through all of the marital turbulence. I would never have researched and studied my Bible so intensely had I never been in these extremely painful situations. My circumstances also necessitated an investigation into my religious fears associated with divorce and remarriage. It was during my failures that I had finally understood what Jesus truly accomplished on the Cross for me. I was genuinely saved, I was a woman of faith, and nothing could separate me from His love, not even the fact that I was failing miserably at love and marriage.

"What then shall we say to these things? If God is for us, who is against us? He who did not spare his own Son, but delivered Him over for us all, how will he not also with Him freely give us all things? Who will bring charges against God's elect? God is the one who justifies. Who is the one who condemns? Christ Jesus is He who died, but rather, was raised, who is at the right hand of God, who also intercedes for us. Who will separate us from the love of Christ? Will tribulation, or trouble, or persecution, or famine, or nakedness, or danger, or sword? Just as it is written: 'For Your sake we are killed all day long; we were regarded as sheep to be slaughtered.' But in all these things we overwhelmingly conquer through Him who loved us. For I am convinced that neither death, nor life, nor angels, nor principalities, nor things present, nor things to come, nor powers, nor height, nor depth, nor any other created thing will be able to separate us from the love of God that is in Christ Jesus our Lord.'" - Romans 8:31-39 (NKJV)

This became a full and beautiful reality for me one evening as I was reading this passage in my living room chair, trying to find the inner peace I so desperately needed. It was like a bolt of lightning from the Holy Spirit, and it penetrated the deepest part of my spirit. I finally understood. I set my Bible down and dropped to the floor in front of me, and I began to weep as if I were in the arms of Jesus, finally home, after a long and treacherous spiritual journey. It was that moment the "bluebird" within me was set to flight – renewed, free, and full of hope.

It was during this time that God first challenged me to evaluate my heart, my lack of forgiveness, and failure to hold myself accountable. At the end of my second marriage, I was hurting and, to be honest, I was quite angry with my husband. But through my tears and frustration, God showed me I was equally responsible for what I was feeling. In both marriages, I had failed to follow God's lead or to consult him regarding the man I chose to marry. I ignored behaviors and situations which should have caused me to question my choices. I wanted what I wanted, and I forged ahead despite the red flags. I had to be honest with myself, and with God. I was as much to blame. When I took responsibility, forgiveness came quite easily.

"Let all bitterness, wrath, anger, clamor, and evil speaking be put away from you, with all malice. And be kind to one another, tenderhearted, forgiving one another, even as God in Christ forgave you." - Ephesians 4:31-32 (NKJV)

When my third marriage was failing, I needed assurance from God yet again. For many weeks, every minute of my spare time was spent doing nothing else but, once again, reading my Bible cover to cover and praying over my situation. I asked God to help me understand what was missing in my life that would cause me to be the way I was ... always wanting to run, emotionally. It was difficult for me to set healthy boundaries, and I was battling resentment.

Romans chapter 8 continued to be an impactful chapter for me during my second and third marriages. The first verse of this particular passage was the verse my sister quoted at the time I was struggling with my security in Christ. I used Romans 8:28 often, when I needed to look at trials in a positive light. The rest of the chapter is abundant with the promises of God! I began to allow all of these verses to penetrate deep within my spirit, to do their work in my life, from the inside, out.

"Therefore, there is now NO condemnation at all for those who are in Christ Jesus. For the law of the Spirit of life in Christ Jesus has set you free from the law of sin and death. For what the Law could not do, weak as it was through the flesh, God did; sending His own Son in the likeness of sinful flesh and as an offering for sin, He condemned sin in the flesh, so that the requirement of the Law might be fulfilled in us who do not walk according to the flesh, but according to the Spirit." - Romans 8:1-8 (NKJV)

Let's pause here. There is NO condemnation at all. None.

For whom? For those who are in Christ Jesus.

Yes, even the divorced. Even the remarried.

How do we know who is in Christ Jesus? Let's read on...

"For those who are in accord with the flesh set their minds on the things of the flesh, but those who are in accord with the Spirit, the things of the Spirit. For the mind set on the flesh is death, but the mind set on the Spirit is life and peace, because the mind set on the flesh is hostile toward God; for it does not subject itself to the law of God, for it is not even able to do so, and those who are in the flesh cannot please God." - Romans 8: 5-8 (NKJV)

You might think a mind set on the Spirit is a person whose life will always reflect the will of God. Therefore, as a temple of the Holy Spirit, that person will never sin in terrible ways. In other words, a believer's faith and behavior will constantly align. So, if I sin (and we all do), a self-righteous person might suggest that I am not saved or I would be making better choices.

The fact that I worried about my salvation at all ...the fact that I read my Bible, searched for answers, and asked God for forgiveness, even in the midst of the mess I was in, *is* a mind set on the Spirit. Conviction and repentance over sin is a mind set on the things of God. Conversely, a mind that is set on the flesh lives according to the flesh. It is hostile towards God and pleased to do the deeds of the flesh. There is no conviction.

I am reminded of King David, who was considered a man after God's own heart. Yet there was a time when he made one very bad decision after another ... decisions which had, quite literally, grave and devastating consequences. The moment the prophet Nathan confronted him over his sin, David confessed immediately. He *responded* to the Holy Spirit *after* he sinned. And he spent much time in genuine contrition to God for his sinful deeds. King David committed adultery, and yet he was a man after God's own heart. King David was not perfect, but he was contrite. (Read 2 Samuel chapters 11-12)

Sometimes we make bad decisions. 1 John 2:1-2 (NKJV) says, *"And if any man sin, we have an Advocate with the Father, Jesus Christ the Righteous: and He is the propitiation for our sins; and not for ours only, but also for the sins of the whole world."*

This, of course, does not give us permission to do whatever we want. If sinning is what we *want* to do, and if we feel good about it, we are not demonstrating a mind in accord with the Holy Spirit.

Galatians 5:13 (NKJV) says, *"For you were called to liberty, brothers and sisters; only do not use your liberty as an opportunity for an occasion to the flesh, but by love serve one another."*

In addition to repentance, I had to find the courage to set boundaries for those who caused hurt and fear during my lifetime. Repentance was good, but change was also necessary in order to put an end to my own cycle. I learned who I was in the Lord, my value and my purpose. I was a child of God. I was not dangling off the edge of his hand as he was considering whether or not, in his disgust, to cast me away. I am loved by him. I am his *child*. I was, and I *am*, firmly in the palm of his hand, and in his grasp (read John 10:27-30). With that, I could finally find the courage to end a pattern by dealing honestly with my own spiritual insufficiencies which led to sin.

I could go into detail about what happened, who did what, and the manner in which I was hurt, but villainizing spouses is counterproductive, and I do not need to qualify my divorces to human beings. I want to be an example of this to you—talking about your former spouse in a contemptuous way to anyone other than a person who has been wisely selected to help you deal with the emotions and aid in the healing process, actually hinders your own recovery, as well as your spiritual and emotional growth. A person who finds opportunity to speak of a former spouse in a disparaging manner is someone who is still hurting, has not yet forgiven, is holding onto bitterness, or is pridefully redirecting blame. Someone who does this is not ready for the next relationship. There is a proper time and place for those discussions—but in a book, in any public forum, among mutual friends, or those who are not listening in order to counsel you, it is a bad idea. You cannot love your "enemy" by openly denigrating them. It is time to forgive and let go of the past.

I have forgiven those who have hurt me, and it is my intention to respect the men who have been in my life. No matter what you may surmise the problems to have been, I urge you to remember we are all spiritually sick and in need of forgiveness and reconciliation to God.

My journey has been nothing like what I had envisioned more than forty years ago, with the exception of five wonderful children. I went through a great deal of pain, suffering, and heartbreak. There was a time I endured a tremendous amount of judgment and harassment by those in the Church. But the Lord has been my helper and protector, even when I thought He was far from me. It took time to see the beauty that God created from it; I wake up each morning praising God for His wondrous works in my life.

REFLECTIONS

Psalm 51:6 (NKJV) says, *"Behold, You desire truth in the inward parts, and in the hidden part You will make me to know wisdom."*

Discuss or Journal

When you were young, how did you imagine love and marriage would be?

_____
_____
_____
_____
_____
_____

How were your experiences in marriage different from what you had envisioned?

_____
_____
_____
_____
_____
_____

Looking back, what 'red flags' did you miss or willfully ignore?

_____
_____
_____
_____
_____
_____

What were the consequences of stepping ahead of God and ignoring red flags?

_____
_____
_____
_____
_____
_____
_____
_____
_____
_____

Isaiah 61:1-3 (NKJV) says, *"The Spirit of the Lord God is upon me, because the Lord has anointed me to preach good tidings to the poor; He has sent me to heal the brokenhearted, to proclaim liberty to the captives and opening of the prison to those who are bound; to proclaim the acceptable year of the Lord and the day of vengeance of our God; to comfort all who mourn, to counsel those who mourn in Zion, to give them beauty for ashes, the oil of joy instead of mourning, the garment of praise for the spirit of heaviness; That they may be called oaks of righteousness, the planting of the Lord, that He may be glorified."*

Isaiah 61 is one of many passages in the Bible that reveal our Heavenly Father's redemptive and restorative nature. Discuss or write down your thoughts to each of the underlined phrases in the above passage. How do they relate to you, personally?

_____
_____
_____
_____
_____
_____
_____
_____
_____
_____
_____
_____
_____

Prayer: *Heavenly Father, thank You for the firm grip You have on me, and for Your unconditional love. It is non-negotiable and all-encompassing. Thank You for Your forgiveness. Help me to show the same love and forgiveness to others, especially those who have hurt me. I know, even when things are not going well, that You are working all things out for my good. I will do my best to remember this truth, to trust You fully, and to give You praise in every circumstance. In Jesus' name, Amen.*

CHAPTER FOUR:

Who Told You That You Were Naked?

Genesis 2:8,9; 2:21-25; 3:1-14, Hebrews 12:6, Jeremiah 17:9, Joel 2:12-14; 2:18-27, James 5:16

In the mid 1980's, I was 17 years old and cruising around in a big, maroon 1977 Ford LTD aptly dubbed "The Tank" by my friends. Alone in my car, I had begun to experience some independence, and became familiar with a lot of secular music by tuning in to local radio stations. Prior to this newfound freedom, I had only heard this kind of music while shopping at stores, or in earshot of someone else's radio. I loved the beat and the sound, but my conscience couldn't always handle the freedom I was trying to give myself.

One afternoon, I was driving to my grandparents' house for a visit. I had the radio on, listening to some 80's pop. It was nothing vulgar or sacrilegious, but it was not "Christian" music. As I was driving, a wave of fear suddenly came over me. I turned the knob and shut the radio off quickly. I then pulled my car over and came to a complete stop on the side of the road. I bowed my head and prayed in a desperate way for God to forgive me for listening to music that was not religious. I truly feared, if Jesus had returned at that moment, I would be left behind and cut off from God because of it.

As a true believer, I should never have been so afraid. I felt I was making good decisions in my young life, though I had not necessarily been given the freedom to make bad ones. Nevertheless, I was not partying or doing things other kids were doing. Perhaps I thought my naivety made me a good Christian. At that time, you could never have convinced me that one day my behavior would not align with my conscience and I would be continually sexually immoral, then go on to marry and divorce, not once, not twice, but three times. How did I go from thinking that listening to Whitney Houston sing about dancing with somebody would cause me to miss the rapture, to an adulterous woman living in shame amongst my brothers and sisters in Christ?

How did Adam and Eve go from perfection to complete moral failure with just one bite of forbidden fruit? They had one rule. Just one. You want to talk about being overcome with guilt and fearing God's wrath ... I don't think anyone since that single incident has experienced, or could experience, the level of failure that came with what should have been easy compliance.

God gave Adam and Eve just one simple rule. *Do not eat of the Tree of Knowledge of Good and Evil* - Genesis 2:16-17 (NKJV). Other than *one* simple rule, the two were free to live as they wanted, knowing no sin, and in a close relationship with God. They experienced no pain or suffering. There was no sickness, no fear of the future or how they would make financial ends meet. There was no insecurity with Eve; Adam never experienced Eve's rejection. Both had perfect physiques and profound intelligence. They had the entire world at their disposal to enjoy. And yet they forever complicated their paradise with one juicy bite of forbidden fruit. It would have been so simple to listen to God and ignore temptation, but one decision changed the course of all of humanity. Because of a single act of disobedience, Adam had to work by the sweat of his brow and Eve had to experience pain in childbirth. They were immediately introduced to fear, insecurity, sickness, confusion, lust, and every manner of evil. They fell completely away from the wholeness and unity that once defined their relationship with God.

We are all familiar with the story...

"The Lord God planted a garden eastward in Eden, and there He put the man whom He had formed. And out of the ground the Lord God made every tree grow that is pleasant to the sight and good for food. The tree of life was also in the midst of the garden, and the tree of the knowledge of good and evil."- Genesis 2:8-9 (NKJV)

Sounds amazing, doesn't it? When God plants a garden, you know it has to be more beautiful than your mind can comprehend. The garden had many trees that bore delicious fruit. In the midst of the garden stood two trees – the tree of life, and the tree of the knowledge of good and evil. Adam had access and freedom to consume anything in the garden except the Tree of the Knowledge of Good and Evil. The two trees set near one another—one was life, and one was essentially death, that is, death as a result of sin.

"And the Lord God caused a deep sleep to fall on Adam, and he slept; and He took one of his ribs, and closed up the flesh in its place. Then the rib which the Lord God had taken from man He made into a woman, and He brought her to the man. And Adam said, "This is now bone of my bones and flesh of my flesh; She shall be called 'woman', because she was taken out of man." Therefore, a man shall leave his father and mother and be joined to his wife, and they shall become one flesh. And they were both naked, the man and his wife, and were not ashamed [of their nakedness]."
- Genesis 2:21-25 (NKJV)

After God had created the world, and Adam had named everything in it, God saw that Adam needed a companion. So, he took a rib from Adam and created Eve. The two were naked and were not ashamed of their nakedness. Because there was no lust, there was no thought to cover themselves.

"Now the serpent was more cunning than any beast of the field which the Lord had made. And he said to the woman, 'Has God indeed said, You shall not eat of every tree of the garden?' And the woman said to the serpent, 'We may eat the fruit of the trees of the garden; but the fruit of the tree which is in the midst of the garden, God has said, You shall not eat it, nor shall you touch it, lest you die.' Then the serpent said to the woman, 'You will not surely die. For God knows that on the day you eat of it your eyes will be opened, and you will be like God, knowing good and evil.' So, when the woman saw that the tree was good for food, that it was pleasant to the eyes, and a tree desirable to make one wise, she took of its fruit and ate. She also gave some to her husband, and he ate." - Genesis 3:1-6 (NKJV)

Eve was tempted by the serpent, disobeyed God, and caused Adam to do the same.

"Then the eyes of both of them were opened, and they knew that they were naked; and they sewed fig leaves together and made themselves coverings. And they heard the sound of the Lord God walking in the garden in the cool of the day, and Adam and his wife hid themselves from the presence of the Lord God among the trees of the garden. Then the Lord God called to Adam and said to him, 'Where are you?' So [Adam] said, 'I heard Your voice in the garden, and I was afraid because I was naked; and I hid myself.'" - Genesis 3:7-10 (NKJV)

Immediately after Adam and Eve ate the forbidden fruit, their eyes were indeed opened, but it wasn't what the serpent made it out to be! Adam and Eve had been blessed with a vast and beautiful world to enjoy, in all of its perfection, and yet they were enticed to the *one* small thing that could hurt them. The serpent made it look like a good thing, or something harmless, and the pair chose to ignore God's warning.

How long do you think Adam and Eve savored the forbidden fruit before guilt set in and the consequences came? If I had to guess, they couldn't really enjoy it because they knew—even before the first bite—they weren't supposed to be eating it. One bad decision, in just a few moments, led to a life full of hardship and, without righteous and loving intervention, eternal separation from God.

The same is true for us. Let's use sexual immorality as an example. As a Christ follower, we will never truly be fulfilled by sexual intimacy as long as we are using it outside of God's design. Just as the taste of the forbidden fruit, it will always be pleasure mixed with the awareness that it cannot lead to anything good in our relationship with God. The pleasure may temporarily overtake conviction, but guilt will ultimately be present. And the practice of sin, in opposition to God's standards, will bring consequences if we don't confess and correct our behavior.

"For those whom the Lord loves He disciplines, And He scourges every son whom He receives." - Hebrews 12:6 (NASB1995)

This is true even in marriage. Our relationship will soon take a downturn if both husband and wife do not yield to God's will for their behaviors within it. Living together out of wedlock might be fun for a while, but a believer cannot remain in it without conviction. If not done God's way, the fun ends in short order, and the repercussions begin, because God loves us and wants to bless us, and the path we're on is moving away from God, not closer.

How long does it take a person to satisfy one sinful desire, one act of illicit sex, one look at pornography on a computer screen, one act of rage, one lie, or one ill-spoken word? Each of these behaviors might seem harmless at the time. But these small, individual instances of sin chip away at all areas of our existence, inwardly and outwardly. The lies we tell ourselves enable us to continue making destructive choices. Our continued patterns keep us chipping away until there is little or nothing left of our self-esteem and self-worth. We think we've got a plan to fix the damage, but eventually, we reason, we've done this much, we may as well continue. What's the point now in doing things differently?

This mindset, without God-fearing spiritual discipline, is why so many professing believers engage in sexual sin outside of marriage or wind up in relationships with people they shouldn't be dating in the first place. This way of thinking is why we have negative influences in our life that shouldn't be there. This is why we hide from God and still can't say "no" to someone who is saying all the right things. We don't like the alternative. It's contrary to what we believe our needs and desires to be. God's expectations do not align with what we desire for ourselves.

Taking responsibility for your decisions does not make you at fault for any abuse or mistreatment you suffered. God loves you, and he abhors whatever pain and suffering you have been through as a result of the actions of someone who was supposed to love and protect you. Some of you will say you did everything right and still married the wrong person. You prayed about it. You didn't see red flags. Your relationship was God-fearing prior to marriage. This can certainly happen, please don't misunderstand me. But for the rest...

There is another way. Let's go back ... way back ... to the time before any of your relationships began...

Just like the fear I felt as a teenager, something was amiss. Personally, I was not only afraid of God, I was afraid of failing my father. I was afraid of rejection. I was deprived of affection as a child, and desperately wanted to be loved as an adult. Yet I pushed people away emotionally because I was afraid of developing deep relationships. I didn't perceive this as "bad" during my marriages. In fact, I didn't consider it at all. At the time, I could only see the angry and blatant misbehavior of others. But I was carrying around a great deal of pain that was also quietly affecting the relationship.

Perhaps many things were out of order in your life and in your relationship to God. You can evaluate your past in depth, but whether or not you find the answer, God is simply wanting you to heed his commands, do his will, and stop eating from the wrong tree.

Am I saying you should follow God blindly, without adequate understanding, and in spite of what you think is best for yourself?

Yes, that's what I'm saying. Stop eating from the wrong tree. Do this *first,* and start walking by faith, in obedience. You don't have to know *why* you can't eat from the tree, or if God will have a great alternative when choose to obey him. Just stop doing it. It didn't matter why God told Adam and Eve not to eat of the Tree of the Knowledge of Good and Evil. He probably never discussed the reasons at length, if at all. Faith is the substance of things hoped for, the evidence of things not seen (Hebrews 11:1). Trust God! God does not have to outline what blessings will come with your obedience. All we need to know is that we will be better for it, and in the favor of God. That's what faith is, and God intends for you to follow—because there are very real consequences to doing things your way, in the deception of your own thinking. Don't trust your reasoning and rationalizations. Obedience is the only path to a new and blessed life. I can assure you, God will be actively at work in your life, and healing will begin to take place.

For those of you who are single, it starts with a commitment to abstinence. God says "no." That's all you need to know. Stop being sexually immoral. Let's go back again to the difference between Jacob and Esau and take a look at the parallels we can draw from the story.

A man with a spirit like Esau has little desire for what has real value (the same can be true of women). He is not looking for quality. He wants what comes easy, whatever makes him feel good in the moment. No matter how successful, skilled, good-looking, and charming he is, he will never fully regard a relationship with you as something to be pursued and cherished. He doesn't want the responsibility that comes with it.

'Jacob,' however, will put in all the necessary effort because he values what he sees in you. However, you must begin to make decisions from a deeper place than the mere surface of what looks and sounds good from the opposite sex. Jacob willingly labored 14 years for Rachel's hand.

Do not be a "bowl of soup", or quick satisfaction, to a selfish-minded Esau. Rather, if the Lord allows, be a focus of love to a man like Jacob. Raise your value. Set that expectation from the very beginning of a relationship. If he knows you have drawn a clear line on this matter, what he does next will expose his heart. Don't be afraid of the outcome.

How many times have you given so much to someone, and still come up "empty-handed?" You thought he was "the one," and you may have even believed you were headed to the altar. You couldn't imagine your life with anyone else ... Yet two, three, or six months later, it's over and the only thing to show for your relationship is the weight of more emotional baggage.

When will you stop being ruled by your feelings, and start trusting God?

When will you begin to respect your body, even when men do not?

Most people will say that sexual chemistry is important. I agree. But two people know if chemistry is present without resorting to sin. You know what I'm talking about; it's undeniable. With genuine love and some chemistry, the two of you will be better off to practice some restraint and hold off until the appropriate time

For some men, they absolutely respect your decision to abstain, even if they reject the same sexual discipline. They value your character and hold you in high esteem. While they admire this quality in you, they don't think they are personally capable of it (but they are). In your commitment to follow God's plan for your life, you have already weeded out a substantial percentage of the male population who would surely lead you back to the same hole you dug for yourself and God pulled you out of.

Raise the standard, and see what God has for you! You are worth far more than the price tag you are placing on yourself. You are worth the best God has to offer, but he can't give it to you if you're running away from him and into the arms of yet another Esau. Change must take place!

When you work on yourself, when you are in right standing with God, your spirit will begin to change quite naturally. You will notice that your focus turns to the inner person rather than outward desires. Your outlook on life changes with it. You set yourself apart from the common practices and ways of the world. You are unique. Chastity becomes something that simply adds to your character and beauty. You value yourself, and it emanates dignity and grace. Men may give up pursuing you because they can't undress you, but they *will* respect you. The right man, if a new relationship is what God has for you, will see your value. He will be your Jacob. He will know your worth and he won't give up. He will work and will "wrestle" to gain a wonderful blessing ...*you.*

How do we find ourselves in such predicaments? How do we start out with the best of intentions and wind up in spiritual, relational, and emotional disaster? Sometimes it's that we simply ignore God's commands. We look at sin as something that will be good for us, something we will enjoy and that will give us some sort of satisfaction, if only temporarily. Just like the tree in the midst of the garden, with all God gives us, we continue to desire the thing he tells us to stay away from. And we continue to learn the hard way, one reckless decision at a time.

"And He said, 'Who told you that you were naked? Have you eaten from the tree of which I commanded you that you should not eat?'" - Genesis 3:11 (NKJV)

After they ate of the fruit, Adam and Eve suddenly saw their nakedness as a sinful thing.

Sometimes you don't understand what you're doing wrong until you insist on pursuing your own desires, and the consequences come ...heartbreak, shame, guilt, depression, anxiety, the awareness that you weren't loved, but you were used. You are caught in your own cycle, and you continue to make the same mistakes. You thought the fruit on the tree looked good. You thought it was something you wanted and needed. You knew God's expectations of you, but you picked the fruit from the tree anyway, and you ate it. You didn't consult God. You didn't heed red flags. You went with your heart.

"The heart is deceitful above all things, And desperately wicked; Who can know it?" - Jeremiah 17:9 (NKJV)

"So the Lord God said to the serpent, 'Because you have done this, you are cursed more than all cattle, and more than every beast of the field; on your belly you shall go, and you shall eat dust all the days of your life. And I will put enmity between you and the woman, and between your seed and her Seed; He shall bruise your head, and you shall bruise His heel.'" - Genesis 3:14-15 (NKJV)

As with Adam and Eve, the act of hiding their nakedness represents that part of ourselves that is contrary to the will of God. We try to conceal it, but the content of our hearts and minds cannot be hidden from God. We are fully exposed, spiritually speaking. God already took it into account, and just as with Adam and Eve, God has always had a plan of redemption for you, and for me! Yes, even in our sexual immorality, adultery, divorce, remarriage, and all of the ugliness that comes with it.

Yet sometimes we continue to behave as if we don't believe this about God. He is looking for us in the garden, in the cool of the day, to have a relationship with us, but we continue to hide in shame because of Pharisees, the criticism of family, or the judgmental people in our lives Satan uses to feed lies to us, and we wrongly believe we have gone too far! But nothing we have done has taken God by surprise.

When someone asks me how many times I have been married, it is very difficult for me to answer. I don't want to open my mouth and say, *"three times"*. I feel like Eve, in the garden, hiding behind the trees, ashamed, and covering myself with fig leaves.

But I remember the love and goodness of God...

"Now, therefore", says the Lord, *"Turn to Me with all your heart, with fasting, with weeping, and with mourning. So, rend your heart, and not your garments; Return to the Lord your God, for He is gracious and merciful, slow to anger, and of great kindness; and He relents from doing harm. Who knows if He will turn and relent, and leave a blessing behind Him—a grain offering and a drink offering for the Lord your God?"* - Joel 2:12-14 (NKJV)

"Fear not, O land; be glad and rejoice, for the Lord has done marvelous things! Do not be afraid, you beasts of the field; for the open pastures are springing up, and the tree bears its fruit; the fig tree and the vine yield their strength. Be glad then, you children

of Zion, and rejoice in the Lord your God' for He has given you the former rain faithfully, and He will cause the rain to come down for you—the former rain, and the latter rain in the first month. The threshing floors shall be full of wheat, and the vats shall overflow with new wine and oil. So, I will restore to you the years that the swarming locust has eaten, the crawling locust, the consuming locust, and the chewing locust... you shall eat plenty and be satisfied, and praise the name of the Lord your God, who has dealt wondrously with you; and my people shall never be put to shame. Then you shall know that I am in the midst of Israel: I am the Lord your God and there is no other. My people shall never be put to shame." - Joel 2:18-27 (NKJV)

The passage is, of course, directed to Israel. However, once again, it reveals the nature and the restorative love of our Heavenly Father. He desires to fill the voids in your life and give you a new outlook on your future, in your relationship with him.

God loves us through all of our mistakes, confusion, wrong turns, and sin. He showers us with *grace*. Grace clears the way when we are stumbling around in the dark. Grace gently corrects and guides us one step at a time. And grace will find us when we are completely off the path and lost in the darkness of our failures. The Lord will carry us back and return us to the fold. And for the genuine Believer, this happens whether we recognize it or not. When in our hearts we are sincerely trying to make the best decision, and in all of our limited human wisdom we fail to do so, he covers us liberally with his grace. When we are *not* trying to make the best decision, he *still* covers us with grace. We are confused; God is not. When we stumble around in the dark, God brings us light. To God, loving and forgiving his children is effortless and constant, even as we continue to complicate matters.

What does it take to come out of hiding and find God again? When God asked Adam and Eve if they had eaten from the tree from which he had commanded them not to eat, God already knew the answer. He wasn't trying to find out what had happened; he was well aware of the situation, and had been planning for it since before Creation. The conversation, however, exposes something in themselves, and toward each other. "*Then the man said, 'The woman whom You gave to be with me, she gave me of the tree, and I ate.' And the Lord God said to the woman, "What is this you have done?" The woman said, "The serpent deceived me, and I ate."*"- Genesis 3:12-13 (NKJV)

Adam and Eve played the "blame game." Adam not only blamed Eve for offering him the fruit, but blamed God for giving him the woman. Eve then pointed to the serpent.

So often, people are covering their faults rather than confessing them. They would rather point the finger at everyone else around them, or to their circumstances. No one wants to be honest with themselves or each other because we might discover each other's (gasp!) *humanity*. There are consequences to this, however. Honesty and personal accountability before God are crucial to real change and moving forward in a new and blessed way.

But James 5:16 (NASB 1995) says, *"Therefore, confess your sins to one another, and pray for one another so that you may be healed. The effective prayer of a righteous man can accomplish much."*

No matter how your marriage fell apart ... if your spouse was unfaithful, if you were abused, if you were dealing with addiction or abandonment ... pray for those who have hurt you. Forgive them. Then do some soul searching and take personal responsibility for the decisions *you* made that brought you to this point.

I had to be honest with myself. I did not place my trust in God when I should have, and I responded to my circumstances with fear and anxiety. I was spiteful, stubborn, and at times unwilling to behave in the way Jesus instructs. I accepted much less than what God wanted for me because I had not come to understand my value. From the time I was a girl, I felt unworthy of God's best for me. This was not necessarily the result of hurtful things that were said to me in childhood; rather, it was the result of things I needed to hear, but were never said. And they can do the same damage.

Who told you that you were naked? Who made you feel shame? Who caused you to believe you were not worthy of anything better? Who withheld their love and attention? Who continues to remind you of all the ways you have failed? Who caused you to feel shame? Who made you think you could make your life better by ignoring God's instruction?

Was it your spouse? Was it your abuser? Was it your mom or your dad? A friend? Is it you?

All that was needed for Adam and Eve to fall was to believe *one* lie of the enemy of their souls, Satan himself, and *act on it*. For you and me, the people around us sometimes do the work of the enemy. A single lie is all it took to reduce Adam and Eve to hiding in shame, and a single lie is all it takes to set our behavior on the wrong course and to reduce ourselves to the same.

For mankind, God already had a salvation plan in place *knowing* Adam and Eve would disobey. On a personal level, a plan extends to you, and to me, in our individual and unique messes. God desires to remove your shame. He wants to restore you so His glory can be revealed to those around you.

First, you need to come out of hiding.

REFLECTIONS

Discuss or Journal

Who told you that you were naked? What lies have you believed about yourself as it pertains to your relationhips with others and your relationship with God?

_____
_____
_____
_____
_____
_____
_____

What does Joel 2:12-14,18-27 tell you about the character of God, not just for Israel, but for his adopted children (you)?

_____
_____
_____
_____
_____
_____
_____

Come out of hiding. What ways have you acted in disobedience? Ask God for forgiveness and put an end to eating from the wrong tree.

_____
_____
_____

Prayer: *Heavenly Father, help me to be honest about my shortcomings. I know there are people who have hurt me, but I also see the ways I have hurt others, or failed to respond or behave as I should. Help me to focus on my own patterns so that I can bring my life into right standing with You. I will be humble with You and with others, because I know You desire a contrite heart, and that honesty and godly sorrow are the first steps to real change. Thank You for Your truth. In Jesus' name, Amen.*

CHAPTER FIVE:

Lessons from the Well

John 4:1-29

The story of the woman at the well in John chapter four is one I have held close to my heart for many years, as I have traversed through the pain in my relationships, marriages, and divorces, and the sanctimonious response from many Christians. I had often referred to myself as "the woman at the well" because I completely identified with the woman in the story in the most uncomfortable ways. This beautiful event was the key to bringing my relationship with God into a right perspective, for two reasons.

First, this was a woman who had been married multiple times. She wrestled with the same enemies ...loneliness, shame, guilt, rejection.

Second, that Jesus met her at the well, the conversation that followed, and the result of their interaction, are evidence of the profound love Jesus has for me also. I could read this story and imagine that I was the woman He met at the well that day.

Let's read the story. It's found in John 4:1-29 (NKJV)

Therefore, when the Lord knew that the Pharisees had heard that Jesus made and baptized more disciples than John (though Jesus Himself did not baptize, but His disciples), He left Judea and departed again to Galilee. But He needed to go through Samaria.

So, He came to a city of Samaria which is called Sychar, near the plot of ground that Jacob gave to his son Joseph. Now Jacob's well was there. Jesus therefore, being wearied from His journey, sat thus by the well. It was about the sixth hour.

A woman from Samaria came to draw water. Jesus said to her, "Give Me a drink." For His disciples had gone away into the city to buy food.

Then the woman said to Him, "How is it that You, being a Jew, ask for a drink from me, a Samaritan woman?" For Jews have no dealings with Samaritans.

Jesus answered and said unto her, "If you knew the gift of God, and who it is who says to you, 'Give Me a drink,' you would have asked Him, and He would have given you living water."

The woman said, "Sir, you have nothing to draw with, and the well is deep. Where do you get that living water? Are you greater than our father Jacob, who gave us the well, and drank from it himself, as well as his sons and his livestock?"

Jesus answered and said to her, "Whoever drinks of this water will thirst again, but whoever drinks of the water that I shall give him will never thirst. But the water that I shall give him will become in him a fountain of water springing up into everlasting life."

The woman said to Him, "Sir, give me this water, that I may not thirst, nor come here to draw." Jesus said to her, "Go, call your husband, and come here." The woman answered and said, "I have no husband."

Jesus said to her, "You have well said, 'I have no husband.' For you have had five husbands, and the one whom you now have is not your husband: in that you spoke truly."

The woman said to Him, "Sir, I perceive you are a prophet. Our fathers worshiped on this mountain, and you Jews say that in Jerusalem is the place where one ought to worship."

Jesus said to her, "Woman, believe Me, the hour is coming when you will neither on this mountain, nor in Jerusalem, worship the Father. You worship what you do not know; we know what we worship, for salvation is of the Jews. But the hour is coming, and now is, when the true worshipers will worship the Father in spirit and truth; for the Father is seeking such to worship Him. God is Spirit, and those who worship Him must worship in spirit and truth."

The woman said to Him, "I know that Messiah is coming" (who is called Christ). "When He comes, He will tell us all things."

Jesus said to her, "I who speak to you, am He."

At this point His disciples came, and they marveled that He talked with a woman; yet no one said, "What do You seek?" or, "Why are You talking with her?"

The woman then left her water pot, went her way into the city, and said to the men, "Come, see a Man who told me all things that I ever did. Could this be the Messiah?"

Then they went out of the city and came to Him. In the meantime, His disciples urged Him, saying, "Rabbi, eat." But He said to them, "My food is to do the will of Him who sent Me, and to finish His work. Do you not say, 'There are still four months and then comes the harvest'? Behold, I say to you, lift up your eyes and look at the fields, for they are already white for harvest! And he who reaps receives wages, and gathers fruit for eternal life, that both he who sows and he who reaps may rejoice together. For in this the saying is true: 'One sows and another reaps.' I sent you to reap that for which you have not labored; others have labored, and you have entered into their labors."

And many of the Samaritans of that city BELIEVED in Him because of the word of the woman who testified, "He told me all that I ever did." So, when the Samaritans had come to Him, they urged Him to stay with them; and He stayed there two days And many more believed because of His own word.

Then they said to the woman, "Now we believe, not because of what you said, for we ourselves have heard Him and we know that this is, indeed, the Christ, the Savior of the world."

LESSON 1: YOU ARE NOT UNLOVABLE

John 4:1-29, Ephesians 3:14-21

Jesus went to great lengths to reach the woman at the well at a divinely appointed time. In John 4:3, Jesus left Judea to travel to Galilee. Verse 4 tells us that He *"needed"* to go through Samaria.

If you have ever looked at a map of ancient Israel, you might think it was geographically necessary for Jesus to travel through Samaria to get to Galilee; from His location, Samaria was north, and Galilee was north of Samaria. However, this is not why I believe the word *"needed"* was used here, and I will tell you why.

Samaria existed in the northern kingdom of a divided Israel, the north and the south. After the Assyrian invasion and captivity of the northern kingdom, people from various pagan empires were sent to occupy the region. It is believed that the northern tribes of Israel and the pagan newcomers lived together peaceably, and in time, many Jews had intermarried, and children of mixed cultures were born. So, the "proper" Jews from the southern kingdom deeply resented the Samaritans and regarded them as "half breeds". The Jewish people also hated the Samaritans because they had built a separate temple, and Jews in the southern kingdom believed it to be pagan. What's more, shrines were built for worship to other gods, children were sent through fire as sacrifices to their idols, and all manner of wickedness was happening in the worship of these false gods. You can understand why the Israelites in the south wanted nothing to do with what was going on there, and despised their northern Samaritan brothers for allowing it. When the Jewish people in the south needed to reach Galilee, they would cross the Jordan River and bypass Samaria rather than traversing through it, thus avoiding the region altogether. So, in reality, geographically, traveling through Samaria was neither necessary nor likely practiced. I believe Jesus had a divine appointment with the woman, and the necessity of traveling through Samaria had much to do with her.

John 4:6 (NKJV) says, "Jesus had arrived at Jacob's well about the sixth hour," prior to the woman's arrival. In the early hours of the day, women in the town would walk together to the well, or meet there, to draw water. The well was a place of social interaction, and walking there to draw water was an enjoyable part of their day. But the Samaritan woman came alone at the sixth hour. In Jewish time, this is about noon, long after the women of the town had returned to their dwellings to tend to their respective domestic duties.

The woman didn't fit into the social norms. To put this into perspective, not only was she an outsider, she was an outsider among the Samaritans—who were outsiders. She was an outcast among outcasts. She was a woman of ill-repute, perhaps denigrated even by those considered degenerate by their southern Jewish brothers. Having been used and discarded by a series of husbands, she struggled to see anything of value in herself. How could she not take it personally, when other women remained with their husbands and were cared for, yet she continued to be rejected?

Perhaps each marriage was a downgrade from the one before. With every divorce, there were fewer and fewer men willing to sacrifice their reputation to be associated with her. She had become so depreciated that, in the end, she found herself with a man who did not even care to do the decent thing by her, but chose to live with her outside of a marital covenant. It's possible respectable suitors were replaced by lechers and no-goods.

Even if you have minimal understanding of human behavior, there can be no denying that she came to draw water during the hottest part of the day to avoid the other women. Perhaps she was ignored while the women around her enjoyed conversations with one another. (Oh, how I relate to this!) Whatever the case, I believe coming to the well at the same time as the other women would have been uncomfortable for her. They likely saw her as inferior, and she probably felt this way about herself. I'm sure there were plenty of opinions floating around about why men were continually divorcing her. No matter her reasons, I completely understand her avoidance of them.

But Jesus, being weary from His journey, sat by the well, and He waited for her. Think about the beauty of this scene for a moment. Close your eyes and imagine it as if you were standing nearby, looking on in real time. Jesus, the Savior of the world, God Himself, in the flesh, waiting at the well for *her,* one woman, a woman not even the outcast dared speak to.

Envisioning this scene brings tears to my eyes. The truth is, my friends, we have the same love of Jesus. This immeasurable, indescribable love for the Samaritan woman is the same love that will also overcome all obstacles to meet you right where you are, and rescue you from the depths of heartache, despair, loneliness, rejection, fear, guilt, and shame. No matter how far you have fallen, His love has no boundaries, and no limits.

Even as a believer, I could not accept the vastness of God's love for me. Like the woman at the well, I allowed the people around me to determine my value and define me as a person. I allowed others to bring spiritual finality to my situation, believing I had failed and could never change it. Just like the Samaritan woman, I did what I could to avoid my critics and accusers. There was a time in my life when I shut everyone out. I didn't answer a knock at my door, and I didn't answer the phone. I kept my distance from people because I was tired of the hurt and hopelessness that came with their presence in my life. And it was just like the Samaritan woman, in my aloneness, that Jesus came to *my* well, and to my rescue, and He showed me His love through His Word and through prayer. My Bible was the well; prayer was the conversation. In that alone time with God, I was finally able to grasp the expanse of his grace, and that am truly loved by him and worthy of love from others around me, including and especially my brothers and sisters in Christ.

In Ephesians 3:14-21 (NKJV), Paul communicated some of the most beautiful words ever written about the love of God and the sense of appreciation it brings to the hearts of men, and it also is my desire for you as you read this book..."*For this reason I bow my knees to the Father of our Lord Jesus Christ, from whom the whole family in heaven and earth is named, that He would grant you, according to the riches of His glory, to be strengthened with might through His spirit in the inner man, that Christ may dwell in your hearts through faith; that you, being rooted and grounded in love, may be able to comprehend with all the saints what is the width and length and depth and height—to know the love of Christ which passes knowledge; that you may be filled with all the fullness of God. Now to Him who is able to do exceedingly abundantly above all that we ask or think, according to the power that works in us, to Him be glory in the church by Christ Jesus to all generations, forever and ever. Amen.*"

The love of God is so great our mortal minds cannot comprehend it. Yet, I pray that you may rest in it, with peace in your heart, so that you are filled and overflowing with the fullness of Jesus Christ. He desires to heal you and make you whole. He will accomplish His purpose in you when you permit Him to dwell there, first, through faith, then through the acceptance of His love and redeeming power.

THOUGHTS ON THIS SECTION:

_____
_____
_____
_____
_____

LESSON 2: YOU ARE NOT UNFIXABLE

John 4:1-29, 2 Corinthians 12:9, Proverbs 14:10

For me, Jacob's well represents the woman's loneliness and despair. As I mentioned before, the well was a social setting, a place where she would otherwise be making and maintaining friendships and genuine connections with other women, but her reputation prevented her from doing so.

When the Samaritan woman arrived at the well this particular day, a Man was resting there. I'm sure this caught her off guard. And when Jesus asked for a drink, it surprised her that He would even speak to her. Yes, He broke cultural taboos with His request. Not only was He a Rabbi speaking to a Samaritan, but He was speaking to a woman—and a woman of ill-repute at that! His request was only a way to open the conversation to something more important. Clearly, we understand from verse 10, Jesus was not there to receive a drink of water from her; He was there to give *her* water ...living water! He was there to offer her something she felt she didn't deserve ... forgiveness, salvation, a sense of self-worth, restoration, and life.

Going through three divorces did little to help my relationships with family, friends, or the church community. Like the Samaritan woman, I was rejected by those who should have loved and supported me. I could not connect with anyone in a meaningful way. But the more I studied God's Word, I began to realize that, when it comes to other human beings, some things can neither be understood nor repaired. My focus should only be to draw nearer to my heavenly Father and to align myself with his will. I needed to lean on God and trust the journey, knowing He would be working on my behalf. Something I had wanted and needed, especially after a series of divorces, was for God to have complete control of every part of my life, including and especially my relationships.

Jesus did not go to the well that day to help the downtrodden woman develop friendships with the other women in town. He was not there to change the way people saw her, or alter the attitudes and behaviors of the women who might have been excluding her. Let's be honest, those relationships may not have been good for her anyway.

Your value is not determined by the number of friends you have, or whether you are married or unmarried. One wrong friend, or one bad relationship, can set you off the course God has established for you. When you are desperate to feel a sense of inclusion, overly focused on making friends, or needing to be in somebody's arms, you open yourself up to everything that comes with it. People are fallible, and they can be envious, competitive, backbiters, and ultimately disloyal. I'm not discouraging friendships; the right friends are wonderful to have! But don't be hyper-focused on it.

Do not use the friends you have or don't have, or your relationship status, to evaluate your self-worth. If you are single, God's specific purpose for you may be benefited by singleness, for the purpose of ministry, just as it was with the Apostle Paul. Sparing himself from "trouble in the flesh" and enabling a focus on ministry are the reasons he chose to remain unmarried. He traveled as a missionary to Gentile nations, unattached and unburdened by the needs of a wife who would take his attention off a calling that was more important to him than marriage.

I considered my own reasons. If I truly believe God works everything out for my good, I have to accept that God might be using who I am, as a person, to fulfill his purpose for me. I had to consider the possibility that God was using circumstances throughout my lifetime to develop me into the kind of person who would eventually operate comfortably as an outsider. It is something which can only be determined between you and God. However, don't be afraid of singleness or a season of solitude. It takes great inner strength to not only live it, but flourish in it, and it presents an opportunity to accomplish great things not afforded to those with spousal obligations.

Jesus also did not show up in order to psychologically analyze her childhood so that she could come to a better understanding of why she did the things she did. He didn't come to bring her an adoring husband who would never put her away. He was there to give her living water. This would be her path to a new life in Him. He was offering her contentment and wholeness with Him, forever … an eternal commitment, something a man had never given her. What she failed to attain in the flesh she could now embrace on another level, with One who is kind and forgiving … the One who would love her unconditionally, and would never send her away with a "certificate of divorce." Jesus offered her that which would set everything else right by showing her grace, and giving her the love and acceptance she so desperately craved.

We are overly-focused these days on psychiatric labels. There is a tremendous amount of help to be gained from these professionals. I have personally benefited from counseling. However, my goal is and always will be for the purpose of improving my future, and not wallowing in my past. I am not downplaying the importance of treatment, when necessary. However, not everyone has this advantage, and what we often leave out is a conversation with the greatest Counselor of all, Jesus, the One who knows us better than we know ourselves.

Proverbs 14:10 (ESV) says, *"The heart knows its own bitterness, and a stranger does not share its joy."*

In other words, there is no person in this world who is able to fully understand the pain you are experiencing the same way Jesus does. No one can identify, minister to, and heal your spirit in a fuller and more complete way than the Creator of your very being.

You are not unfixable! The problem is we not only look to earthly relationships for wholeness, but we may also wrongly believe that healing can only happen if everything that is making us feel bad would simply go away. God will not always change your circumstances; sometimes the circumstances are meant to change you!

When I turned my attention away from people and directed it toward God in all obedience, when I set my will aside and began to put into practice the things I knew God wanted from me—love, servitude, kindness, forgiveness, trust, pure thoughts, peace—wonderful things began to happen within my spirit as I stood firmly in my faith. It did not come without trials. Change happened nevertheless, and miracles took place. It then became my goal each day to remain aligned with God and to keep that special connection with him. This is the only path to healing.

THOUGHTS ON THIS SECTION:

_____

_____

_____

_____

_____

LESSON 3: YOU ARE NOT UNFORGIVABLE

John 4:1-29, Malachi 2:16, Psalm 103:12, 1 Corinthians 14:33, 2 Timothy 1:7, John 14:15, 1 John 2:1; 1:9, Romans 6:1-7, Galatians 5:24, 2 Corinthians 12:7-10

Why is it so difficult to recover from divorce? Why does it feel as if a dark cloud follows us around? Why can we ask for forgiveness for almost any other sin and the issue is over and settled in our minds, yet the effects of divorce and all of the ugliness that comes with it seem to linger in our lives?

Every other sin is clearly defined. If I conducted a survey and asked one hundred Christians if stealing is a sin, one hundred percent of them would tell me emphatically, "Yes, it is sin to steal from people. It is one of the Ten Commandments. Don't do it." If I confessed that I had stolen something and had repented, then asked if God had forgiven me, they would also all agree, "Absolutely, God has forgiven you, but don't do it anymore! Christians should not steal!" And they would be correct.

However, if I asked the same one hundred Christians whether or not I should divorce an abusive man, or if I could remarry after my divorce, I would without a doubt receive dozens of varying answers. Everyone would have their own interpretation of what is provided in scripture. They would differ on what the heart of God would be in these matters, and some of those opinions may include a sense of foreboding as they warn me about the state of my relationship with God, moving forward.

Divorce is especially scandalous because of the sacred covenant that exists between a husband and his wife. Because they are one flesh, divorce is a spiritually violent act.

Malachi 2:16 (NASB1995) tells us, *"For I hate divorce," says the Lord, the God of Israel, "and him who covers his garment with wrong," says the Lord of hosts. "So take heed to your spirit, that you do not deal treacherously."*

A man or woman who leaves their spouse and children to pursue another lover is treacherous according to Scripture. The putting away of that spouse amounts to an act of violence and the rending of one person, spiritually. This makes the situation especially serious and unique. Therefore, many religious leaders handle the subject of adultery differently than any other sin.

Divorce is in opposition to God's righteous standards, and marriage is meant to be between one man and one woman until death. I would never suggest we abuse our freedom in Christ or become presumptuous with something so sacred and binding.

However, determining whether or not to file for divorce is much like going to a lawyer to file for bankruptcy. While a husband and wife are scrutinizing and agonizing over the details of a final outcome, they have paid little or no attention to what got them to that desperate point in the first place. Their finances are in shambles due to countless unwise day-to-day decisions, and neither of them cares to change their approach to the daily management of their money in order to avoid heavy financial debt. They ignore all warning signs, until a lawyer becomes necessary to "call it quits," and they are looking for a way out of their stressful circumstance.

In other words, a man or woman might ask a pastor or trusted spiritual leader whether or not it is right to divorce their spouse, and they will discuss the finer points at length to ensure they are not committing adultery with a divorce. Meanwhile, perhaps both husband and wife are guilty of other forms of adultery (i.e. pornography, lust, etc.), or they struggle with a number of behaviors that are against God's righteous standards, like lying, immoral speech, angry aggression, etc., and have willfully committed these acts over and over again within their marriage. Maybe they are cold, controlling, or indifferent. God wants them to stop these behaviors also. For whatever reason, no one places importance on these day-to-day sins that can lead to a breakdown in the marriage, but there is great spiritual angst over *one* final decision caused by years of unresolved microaggressions and selfish behavior.

They are the little foxes that spoil the vine. In some cases, people don't have a desire to do what is necessary to change their overall behavior, so they don't place much thought into what God says is right and wrong. But when the damage is done and they are ready to call it quits, they are trying to find a way out without being held morally responsible. They carefully examine every aspect of a potential divorce, and whether it is right or wrong, but it seems no one puts the same scrutiny into their sinful behavior during the marriage, before a fallout happens. Why is that? No one is consulting God about their destructive behaviors; no one is doing their best to sacrifice those sins at the altar. But when divorce is on the line, suddenly everyone cares what God thinks.

I am not suggesting that a person divorces anyway because we all sin anyway. I'm pointing out how much differently people approach the subject of divorce compared to any other immoral behavior, which they probably do not take seriously enough. We all know right from wrong without asking. We know the truth about every other sin without pastoral counseling and without the scrupulous study of related Bible verses. However, we are hung up on this subject, and we communicate a sense of finality and spiritual doom in the process. This is not how it is with any other sin.

Are there varying degrees of adultery? Jesus dealt with this sanctimony in His Sermon on the Mount when He declared lustful thoughts to be adultery (Matthew 5:28). Jesus didn't say lust was another lesser form of adultery. Lust in one's mind *is* adultery. Even if the end of a marriage is a much more serious matter in terms of consequences, they are both adultery and, without salvation, a condemnable offense, just as any other sin. However, a Christian typically doesn't consider this prior to a lustful thought. He doesn't weigh the matter before he commits the sin. It happens. He already knows it's wrong. He will feel convicted, and he will ask for forgiveness, intending to do better in the future. There is no finality to it. There is no scarlet letter to wear. He is forgiven. His sin is thrown into the sea of God's forgetfulness.

"As far as the east is from the west, so far has he removed our transgressions from us." - Psalm 103:12 (NKJV)

Why do many Christians think divorce and remarriage are any different?

Can someone show me in the Bible where a genuine child of God who goes through a divorce for a cause other than sexual immorality is stripped of their salvation and condemned without hope? Can someone show me anywhere in the Scripture where God warns us that we should not escape continued spousal abuse or destructive behaviors such as addiction, and if we do so, we can never be forgiven? Pastors will address the grayer areas of this subject, such as abuse, and they will warn us to be careful not to make presumptions on Scripture or permit ourselves to do something in which the perimeters are not clearly outlined.

However, is not the opposite true?

Should individuals impose their own strict, religious thinking on scripture and cause undue fear in the hearts and minds of genuine believers who want nothing more than God's forgiveness and to not feel like they have committed the unforgivable sin?

I know this can be a slippery slope. However, no church leader or fellow Christian should tell a victim of abuse that they must stay in a relationship that is physically harmful or dangerous. That is not the heart of God. No pastor should tell a believer who divorced for reasons other than what Jesus gave by the law, that they will live in that sin forever as an adulterer, even after they genuinely repented. No one should tell a child of God that if he or she remarries after a divorce, they are not in a legitimate marriage, but rather, living in perpetual sin. That's not what the Bible says, they are speaking presumptively and placing God in a box of their own religious thinking.

God wants us to be clear on His righteous expectations, but also fully assured of His sufficient grace for us. If you have truly made the decision to trust Jesus as your Savior, and you have repented of your sins, there should be no trepidation regarding your relationship with God moving forward. There is so much confusion surrounding this particular topic, and yet God is not the author of any of it.

"God is not a God of confusion, but of peace." - 1 Corinthians 14:33 (NKJV)

"For God has not given us a spirit of fear, but of power and of love and of a sound mind." - 2 Timothy 1:7 (NKJV)

If you have repented of adultery or sexual immorality, even something that led to your divorce, and are still living in confusion and fear over it, you are not listening to God, but to man.

Here is the bottom line...

We should always love God by following His commandments. Obedience is the greatest form of worship, and one of the greatest expressions of our love for him. We should always do our best to *not* sin, no matter which sin we are talking about – adultery, sexual immorality, uncleanness, anger, lying... In John 14:15 (NASB1995), Jesus said, *"If you love Me, you will keep My commandments."* This is especially true of a sacred covenant between a man and his wife. There is no denying it is a serious matter before God.

If a child of God sins, he is covered with grace. 1 John 2:1 (NKJV) says, *"My little children, these things I write to you, so that you may not sin. And if anyone sins, we have an Advocate with the Father, Jesus Christ the righteous."* Again, it doesn't matter which sin it is. There is only one unforgivable sin, and that is unbelief. 1 John 1:9 (NASB1995) says, *"If we confess our sins, He is faithful and righteous to forgive us our sins and to cleanse us from all unrighteousness."* Do not allow the enemy to work through Pharisees who want to make you feel differently. If you are a child of God, you are forgiven.

We should not abuse or frustrate the grace of God just because He is gracious to forgive us. *"What shall we say then? Shall we continue in sin that grace may abound? Certainly not! How shall we who died to sin live any longer in it?"*- Romans 6:1-7 (KJV) So, if you continue to battle a particular sin, stop it! And stop frustrating the grace of God by saying you are a work in progress. Even if it may be the case, there comes a time when you need to finally sacrifice the 'old man' and his deeds, and put an end to the cycle, because it is destructive. God empowers us to overcome it, so bring the flesh under subjection. Galatians 5:24 (NKJV) says, *"And those who are Christ's have crucified the flesh with its passions and desires."*

God's forgiveness doesn't always mean you will just as easily forgive yourself. As a man or woman of conviction, there is a measure of regret that will persist. Even after I knew God had forgiven me, even after I had come to peace about my situation, I continued to feel frustration towards myself at times for the ways I had sinned against God. There were moments I would think about it and the guilt would return.

One afternoon, I was home alone and reading my Bible. Once again, I began to reflect on the things I had done and the terrible decisions I had made. I set my Bible aside, got down on my knees, and I prayed about the guilt I was holding on to. I began to cry, "God, I know you have forgiven me! Thank you for forgiving me, but please help me to forgive myself. Help me ...please, God, help me to forgive myself!"

And in that very instant, this scripture came to my spirit. 2 Corinthians 12:7-10 (NASB1995), *"Because of the surpassing greatness of the revelations, for this reason, to keep me from exalting myself, there was given to me a thorn in the flesh, a messenger of Satan to torment me—to keep me from exalting myself! Concerning this I pleaded with the Lord three times that it might leave me. And He has said to me, 'My grace is sufficient for you, for power is perfected in weakness.' Most gladly, therefore, I will rather boast about my weaknesses, so that the power of Christ may dwell in me. Therefore I delight in weaknesses, in insults, in distresses, in persecutions, in difficulties, in behalf of Christ; for when I am weak, then I am strong."*

At that moment, I stopped praying and raised my head to ponder the meaning, in awe! Just as suddenly as the scripture came to my memory, I recalled that the Apostle Paul had a lot to feel guilty about, and I'm certain there was much he wanted to forgive himself for. How many times have I read this story, yet this never occurred to me! No one knows what his thorn in the flesh truly was. Many have speculated it was his vision, or a medical issue. However, it occurred to me that, perhaps—just maybe—the figurative "thorn in the flesh" was his own unrelenting, personal guilt. Let's explore this possibility...

Before meeting Jesus on the road to Damascus, prior to his conversion, this was a man who was a "Pharisee, born of Pharisees" and he intensely persecuted followers of Christ. His actions caused great harm, as well as the death of an uncertain number of Believers. We do know, at the very least, he witnessed the martyr of Stephen, and guarded the clothes of those who were killing him (Acts 22:20). After his conversion, he became a missionary to Gentile nations. Still, as a convert, he had to have found himself at times in the company of the very people he persecuted, perhaps even the friends and family of those he was a participant in the execution of, or had at least witnessed and supported the execution of.

Even if this wasn't the thorn in his flesh, it is very likely he felt tremendous guilt. Don't you think it was uncomfortable facing his brothers and sisters in Christ, even if they showed him forgiveness? So, if the thorn in his flesh was the guilt of his actions towards followers of Christ, he asked God, then, to remove this thorn (guilt) from him.

God responded by reminding Paul that His strength is perfected in Paul's weakness. So, Paul "delighted" in the difficult things he felt and experienced, so that the power of God could be revealed in him. When Paul struggled, God prevailed. It was God who was glorified in it, not Paul. And this is what I addressed earlier in the chapter. God is not always out to change your circumstances. He is not going to erase the memories of your past. Trials and tribulations in life exist for a purpose, so that God's grace and strength can be revealed in us, so that we can learn to rest in his sufficiency, and so *He* can be glorified.

In your alone time, or when you are idle, sometimes the enemy takes the opportunity to haunt you with your past, to remind you of your failures and how much damage your sin has caused you and those you love. I'm sure when Paul was not writing letters to churches or preaching the good news of Jesus Christ to the guards, he had time to reflect on his own life while he was confined in prison. Remember, when distresses, persecutions, difficulties and weaknesses arise, God's grace abounds. When you can no longer take the guilt, pray about it and place your forgiveness and salvation in the lap of God.

Trust him fully. Your memory serves an important purpose—to remind you that your salvation is firmly planted, not in your perfection, but in the sacrifice and the finished work of Jesus Christ alone! When things are going well, and we are doing right, it keeps our hearts humble before God. My salvation rests in the Lord. I must trust in His forgiveness even when I am unable to forgive myself. And He is enough!

THOUGHTS ON THIS SECTION:

_____

_____

_____

_____

_____

LESSON 4: YOU ARE NOT UNUSABLE

John 4:1-29; 4:39-42, Mark 16:15, 2 Corinthians 5:17, Galatians 6:2, Romans 10:11

When Jesus offered the Samaritan woman living water in John 14, telling her that she would never thirst again, He was not speaking of thirsting in the physical sense. However, that's the way she initially understood it, and she immediately wanted to know how to obtain this living water. In her mind, she thought drinking the water would prevent her from ever having to return to the well because of what it represented for her. Rather than it being a social highlight, it was a daily source of anxiety and rejection.

She said to him, "Sir, give me this water, so that I may not thirst, nor come here to draw."

Jesus shifted the conversation to her personal life, the source of her shame, in order to help her understand the spiritual nature of the gift He had for her. Jesus said to her, *"Go, call your husband, and come here."* She answered, "I have no husband."

Notice she didn't say any more than what she had to. She did not tell Jesus that she was living with someone, unmarried. She didn't tell Him that she had had five husbands. But Jesus already knew. He affirmed that she was correct, she had no husband. Then He confronted her with the difficult reality of her life, the very thing that caused her embarrassment. *"You have well said, 'I have no husband,' for you have had five husbands, and the one whom you now have is not your husband; in that you spoke truly."*

If the man had been anyone else but Jesus, imagine how it could have made the woman feel. In the past, I didn't want to talk about the fact I'd been divorced three times. For me, this personal information was given on a "need to know" basis only. I certainly didn't want someone to speak about my situation out loud. But Jesus did not make the Samaritan woman feel ashamed, humiliated, or defensive. Instead, she was taken aback in a hopeful way by what He knew about her, and she perceived He was a prophet. His words were spoken in love for the purpose of salvation and restoration. It was never about judgment!

In verse 25, the woman said, "I know that the Messiah is coming. When He comes, He will tell us all things." And Jesus answered, *"I who speak to you am He."* Jesus came to offer her *life*, not criticism ...and she knew that! The love He had for her emanated in His demeanor and words.

She knew she had met the Messiah. It no longer mattered to her what she had done. It made no difference from where she had come, or what anyone thought of her. As Jesus' disciples returned with food, she left her water at the well, and went to the city, and told the people there, "Come see a Man who told me *everything* that I ever did. Could this be the Messiah?"

What happened at this point of the story is nothing less than amazing.

In all of her hiding, and with all the ways she avoided people and their criticism, Jesus changed her outlook in *one* conversation, so much so that she no longer cared about all the things she felt made her inferior and of little worth. His love and grace overshadowed her guilt and shame. In a single interaction, Jesus changed her.

Her response was *not* something like, "I want to let everyone know about this man, but I can't approach anyone to talk to them. What would they think? They might laugh at me. What kind of weight do I carry with them, anyway? They probably wouldn't believe me."

She cared about them enough to go and tell them the Messiah had come. She said to them, "Come see a man who told me all things that I ever did." Jesus knew *everything* about her. And even knowing everything about her, His interaction with her did not make her depressed or downcast. He dealt graciously with her sin and she left forgiven and encouraged. She now had hope, and with great excitement she shared it with the people in her town. The people then went out of the city and came to see Jesus.

John 4:39-41 (NKJV) says, *"And many of the Samaritans of that city believed in Him because of the word of the woman who testified, 'He told me all that I ever did.' So, when the Samaritans had come to Him, they urged Him to stay with them; and He stayed there two days. And many more believed because of His own word."*

"Then they said to the woman, 'Now we believe, not because of what you said, for we ourselves have heard Him and we know that this is indeed the Messiah, the Savior of the world." - John 4:32 (NKJV)

Maybe some people have given up on you. Perhaps you feel that others have lost their confidence in you, and you are unfit to be used in meaningful and special ways. You may have made so many mistakes and sinned so greatly that you don't think people would take you seriously when you try to bring others closer to Jesus. Maybe you don't feel worthy. Let the Samaritan woman be an example. Jesus didn't stop her from rushing into town. He didn't say, "Hey, *whoa*! Hold on there, young lady. You can't do that! You're a divorcee! I will let my disciples go into town instead."

Jesus used the most unlikely people to bring others to saving faith. He used lepers, tax collectors, prostitutes, the poor, the lame, and the afflicted. He was giving us a model upon which His Church would be built, and that is a full demonstration of His love and grace through the redemption of the outcast and the downcast of our society; not the pious, but the distressed, the dejected, and the wretched.

No, you have not gone too far nor done too much to be used by God in wonderful ways!

Mark 16:15 (NKJV) says, *"And He said to them, 'Go into all the world and preach the gospel to every creature.'"* Not only is it our spiritual obligation to share the Good News with the world, God has given us the authority and equipped us to do so, without the precondition of a perfect or "uneventful" past. If you are willing, God can use you just as He did the Samaritan woman. She was happy to spread the word! She didn't let her past get in the way of her future and her new-found purpose in Christ.

2 Corinthians 5:17 (NKJV) tells us, *"Therefore, if anyone is in Christ, he is a new creation; old things have passed away; behold, all things have become new."*

After everything I had been through, I realized God was using the mess I had made to reveal His glory. I could now understand some of the self-righteous flaws in our mindsets as believers. Fear and shame were never feelings Jesus wanted for a child of God; they have no place in the heart of a Believer. Yet much of what I felt came directly from those who were spiritual authorities within the church.

It actually took my failures to come to a place of truth. Let me be clear: I am not justifying sin. However, God used my sin to reveal the truth of who He is, and it freed me from the bondage in which I had lived my entire life. Without failure, I would have had no reason to search for answers, I would still be living in fear, and I would continue to judge others with the same misinterpretations of scripture I had been taught. And in that state of bondage, I could never truly be used by God. The Gospel is, literally, "Good News." How is oppression and fear 'good news', and why would anyone ever want to be a part of it? Jesus came to deliver us from the weight of our sin.

Galatians 6:2 (NKJV) says, *"Bear one another's burdens, and so fulfill the law of Christ."* God has lightened our burden, and He requires us to do the same for others. However, that is not what is happening! People in the church are, instead, weighing brothers and sisters down with the burden of guilt, shame, and condemnation.

If you want to be used by God, you must begin by fully embracing the freedom and forgiveness He brings to your life, just as the Samaritan woman experienced the day Jesus met her at the well. You don't have to be a theologian or a pastor. The Samaritan woman was not popular. She was probably not well educated, and she was most definitely not a prominent figure in her community. You can be a mechanic, a teacher, a doctor, a police officer. God can use you to minister the Gospel of salvation to the lost, and minister hope, help, and healing, to a lost and dying world, and to your brothers and sisters in the faith.

Romans 10:11 (NKJV) says, *"For the Scripture says, 'Whoever believes on Him will not be put to shame.'"*

THOUGHTS ON THIS SECTION:

_____

_____

_____

_____

_____

_____

_____

_____

LESSON 5: YOU ARE NOT ALONE IN YOUR SIN (people just think you are)

John 4:1-29, Romans 3:10-12, Psalm 14:2-3, Matthew 19:16-26, Hebrews 13:4, Romans 13:1-2; 3:23, 1 Corinthians 6:18; 7:2

The Samaritan woman had a life-altering experience at the well, and she left to tell others about the Messiah. She was not alone in her sin, and she knew it. She wanted others to meet the Man who had come to save the world, not just her. The people of Samaria came to see Jesus and many believed in Him. Every person who met Jesus had their own sin which needed to be covered by the grace of God, through faith. The woman did not need more grace than anyone else, and she became the instrument Jesus used to spread the Good News.

Throughout this book, I have discussed how people in the church can be judgmental of other believers who go through divorce, especially more than once. Those who point their finger are most often respected pillars of local churches with seemingly enduring relationships with their spouses, a strong moral compass, and a lot of spiritual influence.

But there are others who, oddly enough, may also feel morally superior to the serial divorcee. Clearly, there was a kind of prejudice against divorcees in Jesus' time, even amongst the Samaritans who were also outcasts. So, let's discuss those who are like the Samaritan townspeople, the idolaters and sinners who looked down on the woman as if their lifestyles were less sinful than hers. Perhaps you can relate to the exchanges I have had.

I have interacted with people over the years who profess to be followers of Christ, who attend church, read their Bibles, and pray. They do everything any other man or woman of faith should be doing. However, some are disinclined to marry. Singleness is a respectable choice if you are living in obedience, and not in sexual immorality. However, unwed cohabitation has become so prevalent in recent years that it is even acceptable amongst many professing Christians. It is a popular alternative to the marital aversions of an ever-increasing number of people. Often, they will support their decision with a common fallacy—that marriage is just a piece of paper, and that their commitment to one another is, in fact, a marriage in the eyes of God, even without a legal union.

In a conversation with a friend, we had spent time talking about our faith journey as well as our past relationships. In one discussion, he asked the dreaded question, and I told him I had been married three times. As always, this is not something I like to talk about, even on friendly terms. After my revelation, there was a pause. He was very respectful in his response. However, he was clearly surprised, and I could see he was attempting to reconcile this information with the nice, "normal" lady sitting in front of him. What could be the problem? Truly, I absolutely agree. Three divorces should cause concern. Being divorced three times doesn't mean I'm a cheating, raving head case, but I don't blame someone for questioning my emotional stability.

However, this specific exchange was what prompted me to seriously consider the way people, especially Christians, perceive divorcees, especially those who have been divorced more than once, in a self-righteous and hypocritical way. After all, this gentleman boasted only one divorce, but had lived with two other women since he and his wife parted ways. One live-in relationship lasted as long as seventeen years. When discussing the level of "commitment" he had to his live-in girlfriends, he added, "I am a *very* good man!" emphasizing the word *very*. He couldn't tell me why any of his relationships ended. He didn't know. But his lack of real commitment didn't keep him from believing he was a great catch because he had technically only "failed" at marriage one time.

Think about this! If he had done the right thing and truly committed himself to a woman by marrying her, he would also be divorced three times—or he would have never moved in with her and stopped the practice of fornication. The only reason he can boast one divorce is because he lived in sexual immorality for nearly twenty-eight years with at least two other women, unwilling to do the right thing by either one of them. However, my divorces, and wanting sexual intimacy to be within the sanctity of marriage, meant to him that I was more damaged and not as great of a catch. If he was concerned why I failed thrice, why wouldn't he also be concerned that he failed his own "committed" relationships at least the same number of times, with or without a marriage certificate?

Romans 3:10-12 (NASB) says, *"There is no righteous person, not even one; there is no one who understands, there is no one who seeks out God; they have all turned aside, together they have become corrupt; there is none who does good, there is not even one."*

Paul was quoting from Psalm 14:2-3 (NKJV), *"There is no one who does good..."*

My interaction with this gentleman made me think of the rich young ruler in Matthew 19:16-26 (read the story, if you like). Jesus was approached by a wealthy young man who called Him "Good Master," and he asked Jesus how he might acquire eternal life. Jesus' response was, *"Why do you call Me good? No one is good but One, that is, God"*- Mark 10:18 (NKJV). In His answer, Jesus both affirmed His divinity and leveled the man's arrogance. After the young man told Jesus that he had obeyed all of the Commandments, believing that being a "very good man" entitled him to eternal life, Jesus told him to sell all he had and give it to the poor. Grieved at Jesus' answer, the man walked away, because he had many possessions.

Using this story as an example in our relationships, this kind of man (or woman) will only invest in someone if the benefits outweigh the sacrifice. They want the best of both worlds. The rich young ruler wanted to keep all of his possessions *and* attain eternal life. He didn't want to give up anything significant—or if he had to give up something, he wanted it to be in his control, like a personal investment. This is why

Jesus told him to sell *everything*. How genuine was the rich man, and how important was it to him to have a relationship with God? What was he willing to give up?

Hebrews 13:4 (NASB) says, *"Marriage should be honored by all, and the marriage bed kept pure, for God will judge the adulterer and the sexually immoral."*

I have learned there is a lot going on in the hearts and minds of others that we simply do not understand. God judges the heart. They may be ignoring their conscience for a time. Maybe they bought into the modern "marriage is just a piece of paper" deception. Our job is not to condemn, but to righteously discern sin and hold each other accountable, in love and humility, so that we may grow *together* and mature in Christ. That's what we want for each other, right? And that should be our only motivation as we speak the truth in love to those who are professing Believers and living together outside of marriage, or to those who are going through a difficult time in their marriage and considering divorce.

Let's address the argument that marriage is just a piece of paper. There is another truth revealed in the words of Jesus in his conversation with the woman at the well.

Jesus said to her, "You have well said, 'I have no husband.' For you have had five husbands, and the one whom you now have is not your husband: in that you spoke truly." - John 4:16-18 (NKJV)

First, Jesus regarded each husband as a legitimate husband. He didn't say to her, "You have had one husband, which was your first husband, and the four men that followed were illegitimate and not your husband." He did not say, "You've had six husbands, because the man you're living with is your husband despite the absence of a marriage certificate, because you love each other and live in the same household."

No, Jesus made a clear distinction between the five husbands and the man she was living with. She had not had one husband; she had been a wife to five husbands. What's more, the man she was living with was *not* her husband. The woman said, *"I have no husband,"* and Jesus told her, "In that <u>you spoke truly</u>." In other words, the man she was living with was, truly, *not* her husband.

What was the difference between her five legitimate husbands and the sixth man she was living with who was not her husband?

A piece of paper. A certificate of marriage.

Romans 13:1, 2 (NKJV) says, *"Let every soul be subject to the governing authorities. For there is no authority except from God, and the authorities that exist are appointed by God. Therefore, whoever resists the authority resists the ordinance of God; and those who have opposed it will receive condemnation upon themselves."*

There are laws put into place by every government, including laws regarding marriage and divorce. As long as these laws do not subvert or attempt to circumvent

God's moral expectations, he expects us to respect and adhere to them. This means that God has put into place a means by which a man and woman can unite with covenantal vows before witnesses, or in the manner required by the state to be legally bound. These authorities are established by God. The government exists for our good, and marriage is thus facilitated by government entities as an honorable institution. You could debate this by pointing out the godlessness that exists in every government. This is true for any earthly organization or entity. Marriage, however, is a sacred and distinct institution before God, and he has, in fact, established governing authorities to carry it out.

Jesus considered all five men to be legitimate husbands. He said the man she was living with was not her husband. Nevertheless, Jesus' interaction with the woman tells us the following:

1. Divorce is forgiven for anyone who comes to Jesus in faith.

2. Remarriage is legally recognized and spiritually legitimate, by grace.

3. Divorce is an act of adultery, not a continuous state of adultery.

4. Marriage is obtained via the proper legal course that God has appointed (Romans 13).

5. Therefore, a marriage certificate is necessary to be regarded as a legitimate union.

6. There are no spiritual marriages or marriages as a product of our imagination.

7. Without a legal certificate, the act of sex is sin.

We are all the same at our core. We desire love and we want connection. I won't assume that just because two people are living together unmarried, or living separately but sexually immoral, that they are acting without conviction or without plans to make their relationship right before God. Maybe they are, maybe they are not. Still, there are people who can walk away patting themselves on the back for never divorcing, because they never truly committed. In their efforts to stay ahead of their moral fears regarding divorce, they have actually fallen short, just as we all have.

I knew a couple who had lived together for more than eleven years. This beautiful woman helped raise the man's children from a previous marriage. She worked hard. She helped take care of his family; she was good to him. He never had anything negative to say about her. He was simply not going to continue in their relationship because she took issue with the inordinate amount of time he was spending with his new grandchild. His response to the woman he slept next to every night for eleven years, to the woman who cooked his meals, washed his underclothes, cleaned his toilet, and raised his children, was that she needed to accept that she was no longer the most important person in his life—his grand baby was. She had worked, loved, and given more than a decade of her life to a man who fell far short of valuing her in the way she deserved. He could not see his disregard for someone he should have held in high esteem.

If they had been legally and spiritually bound, a husband who would divorce his wife for a reason like that would be a disgrace to his gender. However, the situation is different because in this man's mind, he's not her husband. He never technically made a commitment to her in this way. Even though they lived together as a husband and wife, he maintained his freedom to simply "break up" with her like a middle school passing fancy. And, of course, this is not an assault on men; the same mentality can be true of women as well. It is not a gender-specific problem; these are simply my experiences as a woman.

You are better than that. You deserve more than a man in your bed who prefers to keep his options open, who may be with you only until he wants something different or someone new, and wants to retain the option to exit without the mess, expense, and scandal that often comes with divorce. For men, the same is true. You are worth more than to be used for money, shelter, and material things. Maybe she won't marry you because she is waiting for a bigger "pay day" to cross her path.

Ultimately, *you* are the one who sets your value, and you are the one who raises or lowers the bar.

In today's world, chastity in singleness is an old idea, and marriage is overrated. For many unbelievers, both are even laughable. However, the current statistics do not support these opinions as a "better" way of doing things. In general, we are not the strong men and women of centuries past. We are weak, given to selfish pleasure, and ultimately give up easily, if we commit at all. In marriage, we are accepting far less than God's ideal in our partners, and we are not taking our vows seriously enough.

There are many views on this subject of marriage and divorce that cause us to point fingers at one another, for instance, whether someone has been divorced once versus two or three times. People try to make better choices compared to this person or that person. Yet, no one is really doing things any better, they're just making different mistakes. And many Christians and church leaders, in my opinion, bear some responsibility for the aversion to marriage that a lot of people have, because they fear the judgment that comes with divorce even in matters of abuse. Judgmentalism and scripture misinterpretations have done nothing but promote bigger problems. I'm not suggesting that we should be lenient and permissive; I'm saying Christians need to be truthful and restorative when necessary. A good start would be to stop enabling abusers by keeping their victims in a state of religious fear.

As followers of Christ, when we are at odds over a moral issue, we should defer to the Word of God as the standard by which we should live. What someone permits for themselves could be a deeply held belief, but it doesn't necessarily make it true or beneficial. So then, integrity is not living true to your own values; it is living true to the righteous standards of God. We should always desire to do things God's way, and his way leads to life and blessing.

1 Corinthians 7:2 (NASB) makes this clear, *"But because of sexual immorality, each man is to have his own wife, and each woman is to have her own husband."*

Many of us are not making better decisions; we are just making different mistakes. We believe we are better off, but by God's standards, we are no closer to it than the next guy. Yet we keep measuring our life choices against one another in ignorance of what God truly wants from his children.

"For all have sinned and fall short of the glory of God." - Romans 3:23 (NKJV)

THOUGHTS ON THIS SECTION:

_____
_____
_____
_____
_____

REFLECTIONS

Discuss or Journal

How has God demonstrated his love toward you, even in the midst of your failures?

_____

_____

_____

_____

_____

Read 1 Corinthians chapter 13. Meditate on or discuss what love is, and what love is _not_. What are ways you could show love to your spouse, family, acquaintances, or perfect strangers? What should you stop doing?

_____

_____

_____

_____

_____

_____

_____

_____

We often categorize sin in an attempt to earn righteousness. We human beings compare and contrast our moral state against those who are not living the same way, but the reality is we are all morally bankrupt. We can be quick to judge without understanding someone else's story, because it makes us feel better about our own failures. However, this is self-deception.

We should, first, make sure our own lives are in line with Scripture. (See Matthew 7:1-5.) For instance, the person who is committing fornication has no place judging or criticizing the man or woman who is going through another divorce. Verse 5 says FIRST remove the plank from your eye. First, get rid of the sin in your own life. Then you will be able to see clearly to remove the speck from your brother's eye. Once we have been honest with ourselves and with God, and have dealt with our own sin, we are then able to minister healing to our brother or sister in the spirit of love and humility.

What ways has this chapter changed your views of God's righteous expectations regarding marriage and relationships, based on the truth of Scripture?

_____

_____

_____

_____

_____

Prayer: *Jesus, thank you so much for showing me that I am loved and forgiven. In response, I want to show love to others in greater ways; make me a vessel for your purpose. Help me to move forward in confidence so that I can minister your healing and redemptive nature to those who are hurting. In Jesus' name, Amen.*

CHAPTER SIX:

A Closer Look

Galatians 3:23-25; 5:19-21, Matthew 5:20; 5:31-32; 19:3-9, Romans 6,7; 8:20-21; 6:14; 7:1-4; 13:5-6, Isaiah 53:6, 1 Corinthians 6:15-20; 7, Deuteronomy 24:1-4, Hebrews 13:5b-6

The intensive research attached to this chapter is a reminder of how necessary the grace of God truly is. Grace cuts through all of the confusion and gets to the heart of the matter. It brings peace to true believers who have been divorced and remarried, yes, even after they came to faith in Jesus Christ.

I recall a time when I was trying to "decode" the Bible on the subjects of divorce, remarriage, and salvation to unravel the tangled mess people make of Scripture, from the Old Testament to the New Testament. In the beginning, it was an effort to reassure myself of my eternal destination as a Believer, despite the sin I had committed. I hadn't grasped that grace had already simplified everything for me. After I finally understood the entirety of what Jesus accomplished on the Cross, I then continued to study to more effectively defend the faith when I found myself in a friendly debate on the subject.

I am a living testament of God's grace. I have been married and divorced three times. To some, I am forever an adulterer. Yet, despite the critics and doubters, I am a daughter of God. God is using me, and fulfilling his purpose in me. However, by their own understanding of the Bible, those who loved me were concerned for my salvation based upon verses like Galatians 5:19-21 (NASB), *"Now the deeds of the flesh are evident, which are: sexual immorality, impurity, indecent behavior, idolatry, witchcraft, hostilities, strife, jealousy, outbursts of anger, selfish ambition, dissensions, factions, envy, drunkenness, carousing, and things like these, of which I forewarn you, just as I have forewarned you, that those who practice such things will not inherit the kingdom of God."*

I guess they never considered sins like wrath, strife, emulation, and uncleanness are also listed and can be problematic behaviors in any church congregation. Many Christians like to zero in on divorce, but will overlook sins which are also clearly listed in these verses. By the preferred understanding of many pastors and teachers, adultery (not lustful thoughts, but specifically divorce) is often singled out, and is the only sin Paul mentions in this passage that will actually cause someone to *not* inherit the kingdom of heaven. Whether or not you are a believer is irrelevant, apparently, and an envious or angry person would not have the same fate. This kind of mistake happens when ministers do not present expository teaching. Rather, they have a long-held opinion on the subject, so they search for something—anything—in the Bible to make their case against you. They will use it to weigh you down with guilt, all while ignoring etymology and context. They will say, "God hates divorce," and stop there. They will misuse the Bible to push you to the edge of a chasm of spiritual fear, and then leave you dangling from it.

In this passage, Paul was actually addressing the Church. He wasn't writing a letter to divorcees so that they would repent before they found themselves traveling the broad road to hell. He was encouraging brothers and sisters in Christ to be led by the Holy Spirit so they would not fulfill the deeds of the flesh. So, Paul provided a short list of manifestations of the flesh as examples. Paul ended the list with the words "and things like these," which means his list was far from comprehensive. It includes every sin ever known to man, in the history of mankind, since the fall of Adam in the Garden of Eden. Every sin! If Uncle Joe is getting drunk and cursing at people, it includes that. If Grandma is a busybody, her gossiping ways would be on this list, too.

Every believer has both the flesh and the Spirit at war inside of them. It is *not* impossible for a Christian to commit any of the sins listed, otherwise Paul would not have written the Church about them. He was telling them that the works of the flesh are things which unbelievers practice—without God, without faith, and without conviction. We should not be like those in the world. Rather, we should put away the deeds of the flesh and grow in the fruit of the Spirit (refer to vs. 22-23).

Since these verses were used against me from the time I separated from my first husband, it was also where I began my search for truth on this particular subject. There was a battle going on within my spirit. There were times I connected with God through prayer and genuinely felt his love. There were also times I was gripped in fear when I read verses like Galatians 5:19-21 without proper context.

It did not make sense to me. I could not understand why a loving God who had called me to salvation and had redeemed me through my confession of faith would then denounce me because of a divorce. If I was truly saved, then how could I ever be good enough to maintain my salvation? Why do some Christians think they get to pick and choose what sins will put us permanently at odds with God, and what sins will be more easily forgiven? What's more, could I die, unaware of the ways I had sinned, and be lost forever because I did not have time to repent? Fear begets fear.

As I studied the Bible and came to peace about my salvation, I began to take a deeper look into the subject of divorce and remarriage.

Anyone who has any knowledge of Scripture will tell you, by the general understanding of most church leadership, that there are only two clear reasons in the Bible for a divorce: sexual immorality and abandonment. Many pastors or spiritual leaders will warn Christians that, if the marriage does not end as a result of death of one or the other spouse, divorcing outside of these two reasons is a serious moral infraction with permanent consequences in your relationship with God. There is really no clear-cut definition to either one of these reasons, however, and they have both been subject to individual interpretation.

For example, what is sexual immorality, specifically? Is sexual immorality limited to actual physical contact? If Jesus called a lustful thought "adultery", can sexual immorality also be an addiction to pornography or an emotional affair? What if the spouse who "abandoned" is a true believer escaping abuse, and the spouse remaining at home is the unbeliever? Can you abandon someone in ways other than physically or geographically? Certainly, two people can live in the same home and not be any closer to each other than if one moved to the other side of the world. These are examples of how we can over-complicate this subject when trying to assess our troubled marriages.

To simplify, there is only *one* valid reason for divorce by God's law, and that is sexual immorality. He did not specify abandonment as a reason for divorce, as many suppose the Apostle Paul had. When Jesus spoke to the crowd in His Sermon on the Mount, He referred to the law, as it was from the very beginning, and He gave only *one* reason—not two.

Let's break it down for a better understanding of what is said in the Bible about divorce, who said it, and why it was said ...

DIVORCE FOR THE CAUSE OF SEXUAL IMMORALITY

"Now it was said, 'Whoever sends his wife away is to give her a certificate of divorce';

but I say to you that everyone who divorces his wife, except for the reason of sexual immorality, makes her commit adultery; and whoever marries a divorced woman commits adultery." - Matthew 5:31-32 (NASB1995)

Some Pharisees came to Jesus, testing Him and asking, "Is it lawful for a man to divorce his wife for any reason at all?" And He answered and said, "Have you not read that He who created them from the beginning made them male and female, and said, 'For this reason a man shall leave his father and mother and be joined to his wife, and the two shall become one flesh'? So they are no longer two, but one flesh. Therefore, what God has joined together, no person is to separate." They said to Him, "Why, then, did Moses command to give her a certificate of divorce and send her away?" He said to them, "Because of your hardness of heart Moses permitted you to divorce your wives; but from the beginning it has not been this way. But I say to you, whoever divorces his wife, except for sexual immorality, and marries another woman commits adultery." - Matthew 19:3-9 (NASB1995)

When Jesus gave His Sermon on the Mount, speaking on the subject of marriage, He instructed that if a man divorces his wife for any cause other than sexual immorality, he commits adultery. Not only does he commit adultery, but the law appears to read that the man causes his wife to commit adultery, and if the wife marries another man, her new husband also commits adultery.

Why is sexual immorality, by the law, the only legitimate reason for divorce? Let's start by discussing what sexual immorality is, in marriage.

Sexual immorality, specifically fornication, is sexual intercourse between two people who are not married to each other. We live in a world that has become sexually unconstrained, but let me be clear: It does not matter how we attempt to normalize or purify it in a "committed" or live-in relationship, sex outside of marriage (the possession of a legal marriage certificate) in any form is sexual immorality, of which we are commanded to "flee". It is sin against your own body. You may think it is out of touch, but what God calls sin has never ceased to be sin. His standard has not become obsolete and it is never behind the times. There is a reason for these boundaries, and we are actually missing out on something extraordinarily beautiful by ignoring them.

"Flee sexual immorality. Every other sin that a person commits is outside the body, but the sexually immoral person sins against his own body. Or do you not know that your body is a temple of the Holy Spirit within you, whom you have from God, and that you are not your own?" - 1 Corinthians 6:18-20 (NASB1995)

In the Greek, the word "flee" in the verse means "to shun". Run from it. Avoid it at all costs. Yet our society has devolved to a level of licentiousness that even those who call themselves followers of Christ are entering into sexual relationships with any or every person they call a boyfriend or a girlfriend, without conviction—and sometimes it is more debased than that. Many professing Christians no longer blush at this sin, but live openly in it.

However, to prevent sexual immorality, Paul said in 1 Corinthians 7:2 (NASB 1995), *"But because of sexual immorality, each man is to have his own wife, and each woman is to have her own husband."*

Sex is never just a fun physical activity. It is the most intimate expression of oneness between a man and his wife. Sex is an emotional and spiritual bond that transcends superficial physical pleasure. It may be "casual" to you, but failing to respect the sanctity of sexual intimacy within a marital union has very real consequences over time. You may even fail to recognize the effects it has had because you have never experienced sex any other way; the effects are present nonetheless. Though it may be enjoyable temporarily, it is not wholly fulfilling. This is why, in the world, sexual sin continues to gravitate to new lows. In the absence of its intended design, sex is superficial and lacking spiritual and emotional depth. When it is superficial, sex may become increasingly salacious. A new thrill must continually be experienced, either with a new person or with added deviance.

Each time a person has sex outside of a legal covenantal vow, they give a piece of themselves away, and the relationship baggage they lug around becomes heavier. The beauty and sacredness of sexual intimacy is diminished with every indecent, illicit encounter. I do not cast judgment; I have been just as guilty in the past. Denying oneself sexual gratification can be difficult for any human being.

God is not trying to rob us of something enjoyable; he is trying to protect us. He wants to guide us to something better. His law against sexual immorality exists because we are completely lost and incapable of finding our own way to a blessed life. Without God telling us otherwise, we are all foolish enough to think casual or non-covenantal sex will bring fulfillment, but it is grossly lacking. In fact, the damage that can occur is evident as we look at the current state of the world, and specifically the family unit, versus a century ago. What's more, the decisions we make regarding sex not only affect us, personally, but they affect those around us, including and especially the person we are having sex with. We may even say we love that person. Then let me ask...

Are we bringing the one we love closer to Jesus, or are we a stumbling block to them? Sin is selfish; love is sacrificial. Love is looking out for the best interests of the other person, especially spiritually. Because there is nothing more important than the state of our relationship to God, we should love people enough to behave and speak only in ways that increase and strengthen their faith. We may say we love the person we are having sex with, but what really matters is what we *do*, or *don't* do, to demonstrate that love.

God wants us to experience sex in the best and most satisfying way possible. Therefore, because of the destruction that "free sex" brings, each man is to have his own wife, and each woman is to have her own husband. Within marriage, therefore, sex unifies a husband and wife as one flesh, and it is an illicit act of sex with someone other than the spouse that tears them apart as one flesh, nullifying the oneness and sacred bond they once held.

Back to 1 Corinthians 6, just before Paul told the church to flee sexual immorality, in verses 15-16 (NASB 1995), "Do you not know that your bodies are parts of Christ? Shall I then take away the parts of Christ and make them parts of a prostitute? Far from it! Or do you not know that the one who joins himself to a prostitute is one body with her? For He says, 'The two shall become one flesh.'"

By God's law, marriage can only be nullified by sexual intercourse with another person other than your spouse. The fornicator has allowed sin against his or her own body by becoming one flesh with another person. They are illegitimately joined in the flesh (without a marriage certificate), even if that person is a prostitute, or someone they've never met before and will never see again. If sexual immorality has not taken place, all other reasons for divorce amount to adultery.

What happens when sexual immorality is not the cause of divorce? What about the innocent spouse who was or is sent away?

If a man divorced his wife in those days, the woman had few choices. The first option was to remarry. Even as the innocent party, this is considered adultery for her and also the man she marries following her divorce, in the popular understanding of Jesus' words.

The second option was to prostitute herself for survival, which also happened. Obviously, this is not something a woman of faith would or should do, then or now.

The third option was to become a servant (or maidservant, which could also make her a concubine). There were very few employment options for women in those days. It was possible, but highly improbable. So, if her husband sent her away, she could remarry, prostitute herself, or become a servant or concubine to survive. Which would you choose if you lived in that time and had no way of taking care of yourself?

At first glance, you might think Jesus' reference to the law in Matthew 5 would make the innocent parties guilty of adultery. In fact, it looks as if the woman who was sent away would be an adulteress even if she were a virtuous and godly wife. It appears the man she marries after her divorce would also be guilty of adultery, even if he genuinely loves her and is trying to care for her after her first husband's disgraceful actions. In this interpretation, many have dealt with a lot of guilt and religious pressure to remain unmarried in these situations. Some choose not to marry a person who previously divorced for unbiblical reasons, even if he or she is the innocent party in the divorce, fearing they may commit adultery by marrying. And as for the wife, by this passage of scripture, wouldn't she be an adulterer anyway, even if she remained single after her husband put her away?

However, the phrase "causes her to commit adultery" is a *passive* infinitive in Greek. Therefore, the man who divorces his wife for reasons other than sexual immorality "is making" or "causing" his wife to be in an adulterous situation because she is joined to him in marriage. This is not in the sense of moral guilt held to the wife's account. God is just; he does not punish a person for the actions of someone else. It is, rather, a situation the husband has created for his wife which could have detrimental effects in her daily life. A better understanding of the phrase "causes her to commit adultery" as it pertains to the wife (and if she remarries, her next husband) is that, by divorcing without just cause, the man makes his wife a *victim* of his decision to put her away. He is doing the damage, and she is on the receiving end of it. She is forced into an adulterous situation. He is held morally responsible, not her. Of course, the same applies if the situation is reversed and the man is the innocent party.

Jesus made it clear that the act of adultery is serious, and bears equally serious consequences. A man who would send his wife away into the arms of another man ...a man who has dismissed himself from his obligations as a husband to care for his wife, for no cause other than his own selfish desires, is no man at all.

But Jesus was not declaring the wife or her new husband to be guilty of adultery any more than He would hold someone morally responsible for any other sin committed by someone else. If I were married, I would not be arrested for theft because my husband was out snatching purses from elderly women. I wouldn't go to prison because he committed a crime. I wouldn't be fired from my job for a drug test he failed at his job. If I had no knowledge and am not a co-conspirator in it, I am not guilty of the actions of my husband, and in a just system, would not be penalized for it.

And yet, if my husband committed a crime, I would be a victim of the scandal he created because I am his wife. I am bound to him. What brings him shame also brings me shame, even passively, as the innocent party. Though I am not personally guilty, he is placing me in a bad situation and "causes me" to suffer negative effects as a result of his actions. People will use Scripture out of context to keep even the innocent in bondage, but this is not God's heart.

"The Law came in so that the offense would increase; but where sin increased, grace abounded all the more." - Romans 5:20 (NASB1995)

During His sermon, Jesus taught that lust lingering in a person's thoughts is the same as adultery and hate is the same as murder. The law increases the offense and, therefore, no one is innocent before God. The knowledge of the law, the increased offense the law brings, and the penalty tied to it declare our absolute need for a Savior—because a proper understanding of the law's requirements renders us completely incapable of keeping it. However, where sin increased, grace abounded *all the more.*

By referring hearers back to the law, as it was from the beginning, Jesus was not clearing up the misunderstanding of the law to increase the burden of those who have faith in Him. Rather, He was leveling religious pride and self-righteousness, and He was pointing to a greater righteousness. By a proper understanding of the law, our law keeping will never be enough. How could we ever consider His death on the Cross to be insufficient? What point would there be for Jesus to suffer in agony to pay the penalty for our sins, including the sin of adultery, only to have our offenses increased with an even heavier burden even *after* we came to faith?

Romans 6:14 (NASB1995) says, *"For sin shall not be master over you, for you are not under the Law but under grace."*

Some would suggest Paul is telling us that sin shall not have rule over our lives. While that is absolutely true, in context with what follows, Paul is actually highlighting the sufficiency of grace over sin and the law. As men and women of genuine faith, sin, including all the ways the religious world will try to make you stand guilty before God, can no longer find you guilty; sin is no longer your master and *cannot* condemn you!

Let's go back a few verses in Jesus' sermon and look at the broader scope of His message concerning the law pertaining to marriage, and why He said what He said.

In Matthew 5:20 (NKJV), Jesus said, *"For I say to you, that unless your righteousness exceeds the righteousness of the scribes and Pharisees, you will by no means enter the kingdom of heaven."*

Jesus' sermon in Matthew chapter 5 was quite effective in equalizing all of humanity, and it demolished the self-righteousness of the ultra-religious, namely the scribes and Pharisees, by bringing a proper understanding to the sin which they denied committing. Pharisees in Jesus' day were good at practicing legalism and redefining sin, and they were also putting away their wives for any reason at all.

But Jesus told them they were guilty of adultery. They were guilty even if they were taking advantage of laws that had been restructured to accommodate their hard hearts. Outside of sexual immorality, divorce is an unequivocal sin and could not be manipulated to suit their fleshly desires. This is why Jesus declared that if a man looks at a woman and lusts after her in his heart, he also commits adultery. He was exposing their guilt by referring them back to God's standards, and further taught that sin, even adultery, can also be an issue of the heart. Their divorces were treacherous and adulterous, and likely began with a lustful thought toward another woman. They were not innocent simply because their interpretation of the law permitted them to divorce their wives and send them away. In fact, they were guilty of adultery over and over again – lusting after other women, then divorcing their wives when they were no longer pleased with them. Jesus was putting them in their place.

"But before faith came, we were kept in custody under the Law, being confined for the faith that was destined to be revealed. Therefore the Law has become our guardian to lead us to Christ, so that we may be justified by faith. But now that faith has come, we are no longer under a guardian." - Galatians 3:23-25 (NASB1995)

Unless our righteousness exceeds the righteousness of the scribes and Pharisees, Jesus said, we will not enter the kingdom of heaven. This points away from the burden of law-keeping, and points toward the grace of God, and justification by faith. Jesus cleared up confusion about God's righteous standards regarding marriage and divorce, adultery, murder, and other ways people might feel morally superior.

I've heard pastors explain the phrase "unless your righteousness exceeds the righteousness of the scribes and Pharisees" as a call to do greater works or to follow the law more closely than the Pharisees did. Any pastor or person who misrepresents the words of Jesus so that you continue to bear the burden of the law without grace ... any teacher who misrepresents Jesus' words so that you carry the increased weight of an amplified law they have designed in their own self-righteous thinking ... is teaching falsely and you should reject this error.

A greater righteousness is, in fact, righteousness received by faith in the atonement of Jesus Christ. It cannot be earned; it can only be given.

Jesus spoke the truth of the law to level the pride of the self-righteous and to point to our need for a greater righteousness, the righteousness that Jesus brings. What it means, for anyone who is in Christ, is that the law has no more power over us, and can no longer condemn us. Understanding His *reasons* for everything He said in His sermon on the Mount, not just divorce and remarriage, is the first step to salvation by faith.

There is one last point I want to make on sexual immorality as being the only legitimate reason for divorce.

A woman who is abused by her husband may finally find the courage to leave. However, maybe she leaves in the most sinful way. Her husband may claim he is innocent and the divorce is her fault because she has fallen into the arms of another man and nullified their marriage with an affair. Though he is not responsible for her sexual immorality, he will nonetheless also stand guilty, as a man, of destroying his marriage. He is responsible for any physical, emotional, psychological, or verbal brutality towards her, the fear and anguish he caused her, and his failure to protect her, even from himself and his own barbarity. The same is true for a violent or abusive woman. Yes, an affair is adultery, and the person who is guilty has sinned and should seek forgiveness, but we should be careful, as outsiders, to not make assumptions on who's at fault.

ABANDONMENT

"Yet if the unbelieving one is leaving, let him leave; the brother or sister is not under bondage in such cases, but God has called us in peace." -1 Corinthians 7:15 (NASB1995)

In addition to Jesus' consent to divorce for the cause of sexual immorality, the Apostle Paul told the church that if an unbelieving spouse leaves, then let them leave. In cases of abandonment, they were not under bondage.

Rightly, religious leaders will warn that the matter of abandonment can be subjective. What really constitutes abandonment? For instance, what if the one remaining at home is actually the guilty party, and the spouse who "abandoned" was fleeing abuse or addiction?

Paul's assumed "consent" to divorce in this verse is not an added law to be explicated with excessive, legalistic hair splitting. Rather, it is quite obviously an example of the grace of God at work when the single law permitting divorce for the cause of sexual immorality cannot be followed. Jesus did not deal with Christian and non-Christian marriages in His day. He pointed only to the law, as it was from the beginning, and He spoke *nothing* about spousal abandonment. God's standard is that we should be married for life. There is only one reason for divorce without committing adultery, and that is sexual immorality. He gave no other law which permitted divorce for any other reason, and that includes abandonment. Marriage for life is certainly what we should strive for. However, we live in a fallen world, and things don't always turn out the way we would like them to.

The church at Corinth wrote the Apostle Paul a letter, which is indicated in 1 Corinthians 7:1, in which Paul says, *"Now concerning the things about which you wrote ... ."* Paul sent a letter back to them. Based on his answers in the following chapters, it is obvious this fellowship of Christians had a lot of questions as to the specifics of God's instructions for them, especially where it involved relationships. I am sure they already knew God's righteous standards. However, even as it is for us today, they had a lot of "what if" questions. They sought answers to *their own* special circumstances. So, Paul's answers, recorded in Scripture, are for *that group of believers* to address their specific questions.

I'm not saying that grace cannot be applied to our lives in the case of abandonment just because we are not a part of the Corinthian church. Rather, since the time of the Corinthian church, we have been faced with other legitimately and equally unfortunate circumstances, such as violence that leaves a woman physically bruised, emotionally broken, and living in constant fear. Like those in the Corinthian fellowship, we take these unique situations to our own church leaders and seek godly wisdom and counsel.

In his letter of answers, 1 Corinthians 7:12 is an example of how Paul prefaced his instructions with "I say, not the Lord," or just "I say." He gave wisdom on these special circumstances which were not addressed anywhere else in Scripture. "I say, not the Lord" is like Paul saying, "What I tell you is not a new law to abide by, and it does not come from the Lord as a law. It comes from me, a servant of Christ, giving you advice as to how to deal with this particular matter in light of God's grace." If he had tried to change or add to the law, he would be doing what the Pharisees did. What's more, he would be contradicting the doctrine of justification he had worked so diligently to get new believers to understand and embrace. They did not need a new law to provide for spousal abandonment; they only needed grace for a situation that was completely out of the control of the spouse who had been abandoned. And that's what Paul was communicating.

Perhaps there were some believers in the fellowship who had come to faith in Christ since marrying their spouse, but their spouse remained unsaved and resistant to the gospel. So, their question was probably something like, "We know what God's standards are, but what if the unbelieving husband doesn't commit sexual sin, but just takes off and leaves his wife?" So, Paul answered their "special circumstance" questions beginning with the words, "I say, not the Lord."

There was presumably no sexual immorality happening in the situation addressed. The unbelieving spouse simply abandoned. However, God does not contradict himself; his laws do not evolve with the times or alter for varying circumstances. God's standard from the beginning has never changed, and when men, even religious men like Pharisees, tried to skirt around the law, Jesus simply referred them back to the standard. In keeping with Paul's message of justification by faith, God will judge the motives of every man's heart, and he will apply grace where he so desires. The believer who was abandoned had no control over their situation.

"Yet if the unbelieving one is leaving, let him leave; the brother or sister is not under bondage in such cases, but God has called us to peace." - 1 Corinthians 7: 15 (NASB1995)

In this verse, the grace of God is revealed. The Apostle Paul's call to peace in the case of spousal abandonment is not an audacious overriding of God's law. It neither adds to nor subverts it. Paul did not have the authority to create a new law any more than you or I. Again, that's what the Pharisees were doing!

So, why do many Christians continue to treat it as such?

This case of abandonment is, ultimately, no different than what Jesus spoke in Matthew chapter 5. A man who gives his wife a certificate of divorce and sends her away without just cause is the same as a man who leaves his wife without cause and disappears. Both have "abandoned" their covenantal vows. One provides a certificate of divorce and sends his wife away; the other doesn't bother with a certificate of divorce and 'sends' himself away. In both cases, it is presumed sexual morality is not the cause. In both cases, the spouse is simply done with the marriage. And the result is the same; the innocent spouse is left alone. The spouse that has been put away or abandoned is then put in a situation that has "caused" her (or him) to be the victim of adultery.

Paul understood the grace of God in situations which may find us outside of God's righteous standards, and his answer to the question was simply wisdom when the law could not be followed. In answering their question, he said a brother or sister is not under bondage, but God has called us to *peace*. Notice he was not authorizing divorce; he simply said they are not under bondage (restraint). How a believer moves forward should be prayerfully and solemnly considered by the individual, and Paul affirmed the believer's freedom to do so.

We tend to interpret verse 15 with a strict view that God only allows the abandoned to pursue peace. It is true, in the Greek language, the words "such cases" are interpreted to refer only to situations of abandonment. However, it is quite understandable that Paul worded it this way as that is the specific circumstance he was addressing. Because we do not want to be presumptuous with Scripture, we are wise to be extremely careful applying similar grace to any other unique situation.

Even so, I can think of a few ways a final call for peace may be the only answer. These may include continued physical abuse or violence by one spouse toward their mate. Perhaps a spouse has an addiction that is both causing financial stress and subjecting their children to dangerous people. Maybe sexual abuse is happening. I do not believe God would forbid a woman to flee any form of continued abuse just because her husband has not, to her knowledge, been sexually immoral. And if she leaves her husband, would church leaders tell her she would no longer be an adulterer if she would just reconcile with her abuser? Once again, the same is true for men who live with violence.

FREEDOM FROM THE LAW

One of the passages so often used by modern-day Pharisees on the subject of divorce and remarriage is Romans 7:2-3. There are many verses in the book of Romans that can leave you feeling condemned by the weight of the law, that is, if the passage is taken out of context. It is important to understand why Paul said what he said.

Let's take a look at this passage in Romans 7:2-3 (NASB): "*For the married woman is bound by law to her husband as long as he is alive; but if her husband dies, she is released from the law concerning the husband. So then, if while her husband is alive she gives herself to another man, she will be called an adulteress; but if her husband dies, she is free from the law, so that she is not an adulteress if she gives herself to another man.*"

Pastors and teachers often misuse this passage, and they will isolate these two verses from the verses around it, preferring their interpretation remain within the confines of their own beliefs. However, context is crucial to understanding Paul's intended message. Without context, the reader, who may be divorced, would feel a sense of condemnation, believing he or she is living in a constant state of adultery. A divorced woman, by the Mosaic Law, would be labeled an adulteress. To repair her reputation, she must reconcile with her spouse, who, by the way, may not want anything to do with her, may be remarried, unfaithful, or violent.

In this passage, Paul did not give a call to peace, as he did on the issue of abandonment. He didn't even refer to the words of Jesus, which absolutely allow for divorce for the cause of sexual immorality. This is not a contradiction; the Holy Spirit does not contradict Himself.

Paul's objective was to use the old law on the subject of marriage to demonstrate our freedom from the law, discussed in the previous chapter. We know Romans 7:1,2 is a continuation of chapter six simply by looking at the verse before it. (verse 1), which says:

"*Or do you not know, brothers and sisters (for I am speaking to those who know the Law), that the Law has jurisdiction over a person as long as he lives?*" - Romans 7:1 (NASB1995)

Because this verse begins with the word "Or", it is obvious that he is continuing his point from the previous chapter. So, let's take a look at how the previous chapter (chapter 6) leads to Paul's discourse regarding sin and the law.

In Romans 6, we are called "slaves of sin" prior to our confession of faith. Romans 6:22,23 (NKJV) says: *"But now having been set free from sin, and having become slaves of God, you have your fruit to holiness, and the end, everlasting life. For the wages of sin is death, but the gift of God is eternal life in Christ Jesus our Lord."*

We are no longer slaves to sin by the knowledge of the law, but we are slaves of God who freed us from the law. (Again, no one is able to keep the law.) We have "fruit unto holiness", meaning our lives should be transforming towards righteous behavior, demonstrating a life dedicated to serving God in obedience.

In Romans 7:2-3, Paul used the Mosaic Law regarding marriage to make this point. Continuing with his message of freedom from sin, we died to the law and have been bound to another "Husband", Jesus Christ.

Without Christ, the Mosaic Law has jurisdiction over us as long as we live. We are bound to it, as well as the condemnation and death it brings. Now, using the letter of the law concerning marriage, Paul gave us a clearer picture of just how binding and condemning the whole law really is. Prior to salvation, we were as bound to the law as the woman is bound to her husband, until death. However, if her husband dies, she is no longer bound and is free to marry another. Romans 7:4-6 (NKJV) sums up Paul's point: *"Therefore, my brethren, <u>you also have become dead to the law through the body of Christ</u>, that you may be <u>married to another</u>—to Him who was raised from the dead, that we should bear fruit to God. For when we were in the flesh, the sinful passions which were aroused by the law were at work in our members to bear fruit to <u>death.</u> But now <u>we have been delivered from the law,</u> having died to what we were held by, so that we should serve in the newness of the Spirit and not in the oldness of the letter."*

I have seen pastors use these verses out of context to bring undue feelings of condemnation to believers when they have gone through divorce, or when they remarry. However, Romans 7:2-3 are not written to judge the divorced, but rather, to illustrate and highlight our freedom from the law, in Christ Jesus.

Marriage is holy. Marriage is sacred. It is a covenant to be taken seriously. We should do everything in our power to obey this command, because we love Him and we desire His blessing. However, we go through these periods of our lives, just as King David, when we are not in alignment with the will of God and we are in need of grace.

"All we like sheep have gone astray; We have turned, every one, to his own way; And the Lord has laid on Him the iniquity of us all." - Isaiah 53:6 (NKJV)

Is it not why Jesus came?

THE LEGITIMACY OF REMARRIAGE

Concerning the legitimacy of marriage after divorce, in my humble opinion, this matter was put to rest with Jesus' words to the woman at the well, as I discussed earlier. Even without specific examples in Scripture, the grace of God towards his children shuts down the debate entirely.

"But to the married I give instructions, not I, but the Lord, that the wife should not leave her husband (but if she does leave, she must remain unmarried, or else be reconciled to her husband), and that the husband should not divorce his wife." - 1 Corinthians 7:10-11 (NASB1995)

In this verse, Paul used the words, *"I give instructions, not I, but the Lord."* Now he was clarifying that what followed was not his wisdom in light of God's grace, as it had been in the matter of spousal abandonment, but it is the actual command of God ... that a wife is not to leave her husband. If she leaves her husband, she should remain unmarried, or be reconciled to her husband. The same is also expected of the husband.

Paul was not speaking of the special circumstances discussed a few verses later in 1 Corinthians 7:15. If he were, he would be contradicting himself by telling them to be reconciled. He was referring to all other married couples, in general.

Let's suppose you do not reconcile, but you divorce. Some time in the future, remarriage takes place. Maybe you were going through a period of time in your walk with the Lord that you had become somewhat complacent or disconnected. Perhaps you did not seek out godly counsel on the matter before you divorced and married a second time, but rather made foolish and presumptuous decisions. You moved on and found love again without first consulting God. Whatever the reason, you divorced, and then you remarried. If someone is trying to keep you bound to the old law by telling you that the marriage to your second spouse is illegitimate, the Bible tells us in a few ways, from the Old Testament to the New Testament, that this is not so.

"When a man takes a wife and marries her, and it happens that she does not find favor in his eyes because he has found some indecency in her, and he writes her a certificate of divorce and puts it in her hand and sends her out from his house, and she leaves his house and goes and becomes another man's wife, and the latter husband turns against her and writes her a certificate of divorce and puts it in her hand and sends her out of his house, or if the latter husband who took her to be his wife dies, then her former husband who sent her away is not allowed to take her again to be his wife, since she has been defiled; for that is an abomination before the Lord, and you shall not bring sin on the land which the Lord your God is giving you as an inheritance." - Deuteronomy 24:1-4 (NASB1995)

Within this law is the scenario of a man who married a woman. After some time, she no longer found favor in his eyes because he found "some indecency" in her. The wife's indecency could not mean she committed sexual immorality, as adultery carried the death penalty in those days. "Some indecency" suggests an offensive quality the husband sees in the woman. This would be the modern-day version of "irreconcilable differences", in my opinion. In Moses' day, a man could divorce his wife for any number of reasons. The husband could write a certificate of divorce, hand it to the wife, and send her away from his house. The divorced woman was not prohibited from marrying another man.

By the law, once a divorce was declared by a legal certificate (which was required), the two were not to live together unmarried. Thus, the husband would send her from his house. The certificate of divorce declared them unmarried, therefore cohabitation was unlawful and unacceptable. The specific reason does not matter; one insufficient cause is as bad as another. But they were no longer married.

Once the woman remarried, the new marriage was legitimately binding and further nullified her marriage to her first husband. She was considered defiled, but only to the first husband. This word had nothing to do with her spiritual state concerning a second marriage, but was used only in relation to the man who sent her away. Even if the woman was no longer married to her second husband, by divorce or by his death, the first husband could not remarry her.

Why not?

It was definitely a "man's world" in those days, and a divorce could have had more to do with his own selfish and sinful desires, since we know she could not have committed adultery. Forbidding the former husband to take the woman back after she had been defiled (again, only in relation to the first husband), was a penalty to *him,* not her, for having put her away for insufficient cause in the first place.

All of this brings me to my intended point: Even with insufficient cause, the woman in the scenario remarried. By the Mosaic Law, the fact that a man could not remarry his former spouse after her remarriage is evidence that God regards a second marriage to be legitimate, just as it was with the woman at the well. *Reconciliation* with the first husband was no longer an option because she had—legitimately—remarried.

Now, let's go back to the letter from Paul to the Corinthian church. I will quote this verse directly from my Greek Reverse Interlinear... 1 Corinthians 7:8 (NKJV) says, *"But I say to the unmarried and to the widows: It is good for them if they remain even as I am; but if they cannot exercise self-control, let them marry. For it is better to marry than to burn with passion."*

Remember a few verses earlier (1 Corinthians 7:2), Paul told the church, because of sexual immorality each man should take a wife, and each woman should take a husband.

Do you think Paul was only talking about virgins or widowers when he referred to the "unmarried"? Or can we all agree that those who have been divorced are also unmarried, according to Scripture, and can also burn with passion? Someone who has experienced the closeness and intimacy of a physical, sexual union could struggle with celibacy more than a virgin would. From the preferred translation, however, there are only certain people who are permitted to remarry to prevent sexual immorality. The rest can just burn with passion for the rest of their mortal days. However, if it is for sexual immorality that a man should take a wife, and vice versa, why does this not include those who have been divorced and forgiven by grace?

Read a few commentaries on 1 Corinthians 7:8 and you will see Bible scholars skirt around the possibility of verse 8 referring also to the unmarried by way of divorce. Many will say the word "unmarried" refers to virgins or widows only, even though there is no real evidence to support its limitation to one or the other group alone.

The Greek word for unmarried, and the word used in this verse, is *agamos*. It refers to all unmarried adults, and it is, in fact, also the same word used for singleness as a result of divorce. If you are unmarried, whether you are a virgin, a widower, or a divorcee, the word is *agamos,* male or female. As such, the correct interpretation for the word "unmarried" in this verse is anyone who is not currently married. Paul used a general term here. If he wished to deny remarriage to the divorced and give them no means to "flee" sexual immorality, he would have specified.

The Apostle Paul encouraged singleness for those who were unmarried. Personally, I think this advice is especially wise for the divorced. He said it was good to remain unmarried, as he was. Marriage brings "trouble in the flesh", and it keeps us from fully devoting ourselves to ministry because we are also concerned with taking care of and supporting our spouse, or we get caught up in and distracted with conflict that comes with it.

No matter the reason for a state of singleness, if someone is "burning with passion" and lacks the spiritual discipline to remain celibate, the obvious solution would be to find a companion and remarry so that their conscience can be at peace. Again, 1 Corinthians 7:2 (NKJV) says, *"Nevertheless, because of sexual immorality, let each man have his own wife, and let each woman have her own husband."*

However, any view of limited grace in these circumstances offers no peace at all for the divorced. If they remain unmarried, they may struggle with loneliness and celibacy. If they remarry, they may experience feelings of guilt and fear because they did not divorce for just cause, sexual immorality. This is much of the reason many people refuse to marry at all, believing that continuing in a state of sexual immorality (mentally or physically) is somehow morally preferable to being married or remarried, for fear of God's judgment. I understand the concern of church leaders, but there was a time I was unable to settle the matter in my conscience, between the Holy Spirit and me, because the religious pride in others wouldn't permit it, and they continued to deny me the grace that God had already freely given.

To the divorced, it is very important that you consider your reasons for remarriage and strive to keep your heart pure before the Lord. If you have been sexually immoral, repent, and know that God is faithful to forgive his children. I am not saying we should act with presumption of grace; all I am saying is, when you have sinned, God is gracious and forgives us. Keep your heart and motives in check at all times, because that is what God judges.

Place every sin under the Blood of Jesus Christ through confession, and doing everything in our power to follow God's direction. We may mess things up, and then sin again. God is faithful and just to forgive us of all—ALL—unrighteousness! If you belong to God, you will overcome! It may not be in the preferred timing of the religious people around you, but you will bear fruit of righteousness despite your failures.

As a single woman, now divorced three times, I have surrendered my future to God completely. It is no longer my will, but God's. I don't want to fill that void with anything else but Jesus. I sought him out many years ago on this subject, so that I could come to a place of healing and better understanding of His character. As a genuine child of God, learning about my freedom in Christ ultimately did not embolden me to embrace a sinful lifestyle. In the end, it did just the opposite. Fear imprisoned me. Religious bondage actually kept me in a cycle of sin because I saw no hope. But freedom in Christ released me to do more for his glory.

For most of my adult life, I was afraid and always pleading for mercy. I slowly discovered the truth of His love for me. It took me years to de-program the belief system I had grown up with, and then years longer to accept that God truly does forgive me. Yes, God has even forgiven my adultery. I finally fully realized and embraced His love for me. With it has come some necessary chastisement, but the end has brought tremendous spiritual growth, a better heart, a more genuine relationship with God, and as a result, better relationships with those around me. Press in, search for answers, call on God to fill the voids in your life. Get to know His Word!

Romans 5:20-21 (NKJV) says, *"Moreover the law entered that the offense might abound. But where sin abounded, grace abounded much more, so that as sin reigned in death, even so grace might reign through righteousness to eternal life through Jesus Christ our Lord."*

Remember the law? The thing that tells me I am to be called an adulteress? Grace abounded all the more, and I am called a child of God.

Here is the verse I am following in this season of singleness. *"A wife is bound as long as her husband lives; but if her husband is dead, she is free to be married to whom she wishes, only in the Lord. But in my opinion she is happier if she remains as she is; and I think that I also have the Spirit of God."* -1 Corinthians 7:39-40 (NASB1995)

For men and women who are facing the world alone, it really doesn't matter what your reasons are for being single. Maybe your spouse is deceased. Maybe you are divorced, or perhaps you never married. Paul said at the end of this verse, in his opinion, the single woman is happier if she remains as she is, and he also felt he had the Spirit of God in this thought. If the Apostle Paul believed he had the Spirit of God in that thought, that's good enough for me! Why wouldn't you want to try God rather than continue to look to another human being for completeness? Lean into God, and try him.

Don't be afraid to find happiness in singleness, if it is what the Lord desires for you. Ask God to fill that void in your life. Appeal to him to give you the means, the strength, and the confidence you need to face any challenges that come your way. God is with you. He is your protector. You may have experienced abandonment, abuse, disloyalty, fear, and heartache in your marriage(s), but God will never leave nor forsake you! I love how it is written in Hebrews 13:5b-6 (NASB 1995), *"...for He Himself has said, 'I will never desert you, nor will I ever abandon you,' so that we confidently say, 'The Lord is my helper, I will not be afraid. What will man do to me?'"*

REFLECTIONS

I hope by this point in the book, you have come to a better understanding of what the Bible has to say on the subject of divorce and remarriage. It is my goal to communicate five things:

1. The sanctity of marriage, and God's expectation that it lasts a lifetime.

2. As such, we commit our ways to the Lord in our marriage, and surrender to his will.

3. When divorce becomes a possibility, we should obey God by pursuing reconciliation.

4. If divorce happens, as a child of God, we have an Advocate, and He will forgive us.

5. If remarriage is an option, we prayerfully seek God's will rather than our own desires, even if it means to remain unmarried.

Romans 14:22-23 (NASB1995) says, *"The faith which you have, have as your own conviction before God. Blessed is the one who does not condemn himself in what he approves. But the one who doubts is condemned if he eats, because his eating is not from faith; and whatever is not from faith is sin."*

The Apostle Paul was dealing with issues concerning holy days, meat, and drink among Believers. However, on the subject of divorce and remarriage, the message is the same. You should never violate your own deeply-held beliefs! If it causes guilt, it should not be done. Do not violate your conscience.

Your moral obligation is to maintain a clear conscience before God on matters in which the "what ifs" are not explicitly addressed in Scripture. This is not to minimize divorce and remarriage by likening it to whether or not we should eat meat that has been sacrificed to idols, or if we should drink wine, watch a movie in the theater, pierce our ears, or get tattoos. A covenant between two people is much more serious than these legalistic matters. Still, the issue can become complex because there are so many variables and the details are so personal. It can result in inner conflict. Even after seeking godly counsel, our next move should always be in the fear of the Lord and in light of what he is speaking to us about our very personal situation, through the Word and through much prayer.

"One person values one day over another, another values every day the same. Each person must be fully convinced in his own mind."- Romans 14:5 (NASB1995)

"So then each one of us will give an account of himself to God." - Romans 14:12 (NASB1995)

"Therefore let's not judge one another anymore, but rather determine this: not to put an obstacle or a stumbling block in a brother's way." - Romans 14:13 (NASB1995)

My objective is to bring those who feel guilt and shame, or feel condemned by any Christian, to a proper understanding of Scripture, so that the abused, downtrodden, outcast, and hurting may find peace and experience the reality of God's love and forgiveness for his children. My goal is not to give you permission to do those things which are in contradiction to your conscience; you should not do them either.

First, consider your own conscience on your personal situation, in light of the Word:

_____

_____

_____

_____

_____

Next, if you have gone through a divorce, or multiple divorces, you need a plan moving forward. If you are remarried, pray and ask God about what you can do to improve your marriage. This is not about your spouse, or what he or she is doing or not doing. Taking personal responsibility for keeping a marriage together will require some serious introspection, honesty, humility, and sacrifice.

Journal or discuss your thoughts on the changes you should make as you move forward:

_____

_____

_____

_____

_____

Finally, if you are divorced and unmarried, reflect on how you might use this time of singleness to prepare for the potential of a future relationship. What changes should you be making? In what ways do you need to heal in order to give anyone in your future the best version of yourself?

_____

_____

_____

_____

_____

Prayer: _Heavenly Father, thank you for your Word. Please give me the strength to lay aside my own desires and follow after your will for me. Guide me in all wisdom, and help me to follow in your footsteps as you direct. Give me the humility I need to look inwardly in an honest way so that I can end any cycles that are harmful or destructive to me and to my relationships as I move forward. As I respond in obedience, open new doors for me with increased ministry and purpose in the building of your kingdom. In Jesus' name, Amen._

CHAPTER SEVEN:

Victim or Victor: Steps to Overcoming

2 Corinthians 4:8-9, 16-18, James 1:2-4; Romans 5:3-5, Proverbs 18:24;
Deuteronomy 31:6, Colossians 3:23; Galatians 6:9, Matthew 10:29-31; Romans
8:35, 1 Peter 5:10; Psalm 30:5. John 16:33

Any time I had a defeatist attitude, my dad would ask me, "*Are you a victim or a victor?*" He would encourage me with verses like Philippians 4:13, "I can do *all* things through Christ, Who gives me strength." He would remind me that God has not given me the spirit of fear, but of power, love, and a sound mind, (2 Timothy 1:7), and to be anxious for nothing, (Philippians 4:6). It was difficult to put these biblical truths into practice when so much of my young life was ruled by religious fear.

It's easy to quote verses and say we believe them ... but do we? When trying to attain victory over guilt, fear, and sin, it is vital to know the truth, to believe it, then put it into practice through faith.

"And you will know the truth, and the truth will make you free."- John 8:32 (NASB1995

It's also important to remember how much Jesus loves you, and that He is waiting for you at your own well—your heart—to minister healing, to give you hope and a new start.

"He heals the brokenhearted and binds up their wounds." - Psalm 147:3 (NKJV)

"The Lord is near to the brokenhearted, And saves those who are crushed in spirit. The afflictions of the righteous are many, but the Lord rescues him from them all." - Psalm 34:18-19 (NASB1995)

"Come to Me, all who are weary and burdened, and I will give you rest. Take My yoke upon you and learn from Me, for I am gentle and humble in heart, and you will find rest for your souls. For My yoke is comfortable, and My burden is light." - Matthew

11:28-30 (NASB1995)

Jesus is intimately familiar with you, every detail, and in every way. He is our best source of help and healing, in the deepest part of our spirit. And when Jesus is in control, He will have some expectations of you.

KEEP THE PAIN IN PERSPECTIVE

"We are afflicted in every way, but not crushed; perplexed, but not despairing; persecuted, but not abandoned; struck down, but not destroyed; Therefore we do not lose heart, but though our outer person is decaying, yet our inner person is being renewed day by day. For our momentary, light affliction is producing for us an eternal weight of glory far beyond all comparison, while we look not at the things which are seen, but at the things which are not seen; for the things which are seen are temporal, but the things which are not seen are eternal." - 2 Corinthians 4:8-9, 16-18 (NASB1995)

As a missionary to Gentile nations, Paul suffered many trials and tribulations for the sake of the Gospel. In this passage, he is a model of what it means to endure earthly suffering. We learn from Paul that, no matter what we have been through, it is momentary, and it is immaterial in light of eternity.

What's more, Paul had a "the glass is half full" mindset. He said they were afflicted. Even so, they were not crushed. They were despairing, but at least they weren't abandoned. They were struck down, but thank God, they were not destroyed!

God has not abandoned us, and he has not struck us down. He never leaves us. In our suffering, we await eternal glory, far beyond anything we could ever imagine. It gives us every reason to *rejoice*!

CONSIDER THE POSITIVE

"Consider it all joy, my brothers and sisters, when you encounter various trials, knowing that the testing of your faith produces endurance. And let endurance have its perfect result, so that you may be perfect and complete, lacking in nothing." - James 1:2-4 (NASB1995)

"And not only this, but we also celebrate in our tribulations, knowing that tribulation brings about perseverance; and perseverance, proven character; and proven character, hope; and hope does not disappoint, because the love of God has been poured out within our hearts through the Holy Spirit who was given to us." - Romans 5:3-5 (NASB1995)

James told us to consider it all joy when we encounter trials, and Paul told us to celebrate them!

Looking back, not only did God help me through my trials and tribulations, he also brought good into my life as a result. It produced in me forgiveness, compassion, gentleness, strength of character, hope, perseverance, and so much more. We cannot grow to be strong in the Lord without trials and tribulations. They are the opportunities we need to develop into mature Christians. They are tests given to us to produce godly character, to gain eternal rewards, and to open the door to blessings. Even in the midst of our pain, may we remember that God is with us. May we see the positive—that our trials are a gift, an opportunity to face the challenges with grace and gratitude.

YOU HAVE THE ONLY FRIEND YOU NEED

"A person with too many friends comes to ruin, But there is a friend who sticks closer than a brother." - Proverbs 18:24 (NASB1995)

"Be strong and courageous, do not be afraid or in dread of them, for the Lord your God is the One who is going with you. He will not desert you or abandon you." - Deuteronomy 31:6 (NASB1995)

You are never alone. I wake up each morning talking to Jesus. I know He is listening. I thank Him for what He has done in my life. I talk to Him about what is bothering me, and ask Him to lead me in the right direction, and to keep my heart pure. A human friend will respond to us in ways that can be physically felt and heard, with a hug and a verbal, "I'm here for you." Maybe the reason we fail to try Jesus as our truest and dearest friend is because we limit Him by comparing Him to the tangible and immediate comfort of the human response. But He is so much bigger and greater than that, and is able to do exceedingly abundantly above all that we ask or think! (Read Ephesians 3:20-21.)

I am not suggesting that we do not need friends. We should absolutely find real connection within the household of faith. Building a community of spiritual support and friendship around us is very important. However, at times that we feel alone, the friendship of Jesus is enduring, and it can be felt in the whole of our existence, in every facet of our lives. It is not limited to the consoling words of those who are ultimately powerless to soften the hearts of our enemies or change our circumstances. Earthly friends are limited, but Jesus is Lord, and if there is One we can call on for the right kind of help, it is our Creator.

KEEP GIVING

"Whatever you do, do your work heartily, as for the Lord rather than for men." - Colossians 3:23 (NASB1995)

"Let's not become discouraged in doing good, for in due time we will reap, if we do not become weary." - Galatians 6:9 (NASB1995)

Being of service to our fellow man temporarily takes the focus off our circumstances and directs our attention to showing the love of Christ to others. Find ministries and outreaches to be involved in, or positions of service within the church, preferably in an area that God has gifted you, and in something that you can be excited about! Your gifts have been given to you to glorify God and to bless others. If you are a musician, start a band or get involved with the worship team at church. If you are good with kids, perhaps you have thought about fostering children or being a part of a children's ministry. You can volunteer at a homeless shelter or start a Bible study group in your home. If you are a mechanic, maybe you can offer free oil changes to a few single mothers each month.

When we do it as unto the Lord, we are not looking for the other person (or people) to reciprocate or to respond to our gestures of kindness as we think they should. Rather, the promise of return is appropriately shifted from the recipient of our giving to our unfailing heavenly Father. Our giving is never to be with an expectation of return anyway. There is healing in the act of giving, and God will bless you for it.

KNOW WHO YOU ARE TO JESUS

"Are not two sparrows sold for a cent? And yet not one of them will fall to the ground apart from your Father. But the very hairs of your head are all numbered. So do not fear; you are more valuable than many sparrows." - Matthew 10:29-31 (NASB1995)

"Who will separate us from the love of Christ? Will tribulation, or distress, or persecution, or famine, or nakedness, or peril, or sword?" - Romans 8:35 (NASB1995)

Jesus told us in Matthew 10, above, that two sparrows are sold for an assarion. An assarion is like a farthing or a penny. As near worthless as sparrows are to people, not one sparrow falls to the ground without the Lord's knowledge.

How much more important to Jesus are we than a sparrow, or a great number of sparrows? If He sees what befalls one sparrow, does the Lord not also pay attention to every intricate detail of our lives? Do we really trust His providence? He is so intimately involved, He even knows the number of hairs on our head. We are constantly losing and growing hair, so how can we not be amazed at how closely He is watching us each and every moment!

And if the Lord knows the number of our hairs, don't you think He is also familiar with and acutely aware of our sadness and pain?

This thought alone should bring us to our knees, overwhelmed with the knowledge of who we are to the Savior. How could we not desire to be ever closer to Him?

REMEMBER GOD'S PROMISE OF JOY

"But may the God of all grace, who called us to His eternal glory by Christ Jesus, after you have suffered a while, perfect, establish, strengthen, and settle you." - 1 Peter 5:10 (NKJV)

"For His anger is but for a moment, His favor is for life; Weeping may endure for a night, but joy comes in the morning." - Psalm 30:5 (NKJV)

Every horrible thing we go through in this world is only temporary ... every episode of abuse, every bit of pain we feel from marital unfaithfulness, every feeling of shame or guilt, every breakup we suffer, every disease or death of a loved one we endure. Someday, when Jesus returns, there will be no more sickness, no more pain, and no more sorrow. We can cling to this hope, and it brings us comfort in times we recall our sufferings.

THERE IS VICTORY IN JESUS

"These things I have spoken to you, that in Me you may have peace. In the world you will have tribulation; but be of good cheer, I have overcome the world." - John 16:33 (NKJV)

Now divorced three times, I made a decision to fully embrace singleness for as long as I am called to it. I fought the desire to be sexually immoral. I accomplished what the Lord had required of me in loving and taking care of my stepmother after my father's death, and forgiving those who had hurt me. I decided to fully "put on" Christ, in every way ... in my attitude, my speech, and my mindset. Whatever He instructed, that's what I would do. Even in trials, my life changed for the better, and God has done many wonderful works in it.

REFLECTIONS

For each point, discuss or write about what actions you will take to move forward in your life with the mindset of a victor...

KEEP THE PAIN IN PERSPECTIVE:

_____
_____
_____
_____
_____

CONSIDER THE POSITIVE:

_____
_____
_____
_____
_____

YOU HAVE THE ONLY FRIEND YOU NEED:

_____
_____
_____
_____
_____

KEEP GIVING:

_____
_____
_____
_____
_____

KNOW WHO YOU ARE TO JESUS:

_____
_____
_____
_____
_____

REMEMBER GOD'S PROMISE OF JOY:

_____
_____
_____
_____
_____

THERE IS VICTORY IN JESUS:

_____
_____
_____
_____
_____
_____

Prayer: *Heavenly Father, thank You for allowing me to see that, no matter how bad things seem to get in my life, You are always with me. Please help me to always stay focused on the positive because, in You, I am truly a victor! I am blessed to know You are intimately familiar with every detail of my life and are working through my trials with me to make me more like You. Open doors of opportunity as I search for ways to serve and give to others. In Jesus' name, Amen.*

CHAPTER EIGHT:

To Judge, or not to Judge, that is the Question

A Plea to Christ Followers

John 7:23-24, Romans 14:10-13; 15:1-6, Galatians 6:1, Matthew 7:1-5

I dislike having to tell people I've been divorced, much less three times. However, in the company of budding relationships (friendships and otherwise), the subject is bound to come up sooner or later. In the past, if the truth had to be spoken, I felt I also needed to disclose *why* my marriages had failed. I wanted to put an end to the judgment I believed was already taking place in their minds. I thought I would be the woman that others with loving, committed husbands would never want to befriend. After all, I must have issues, right? No matter how put together I looked on the outside, I must be a freaking mess beneath my latest fashion purchases, number 140 lipstick, and meticulously-styled hair.

When someone asked, I would share my subjectively honest reasons to establish myself as an otherwise emotionally healthy and mentally stable person who was simply unlucky in love. I had gotten pretty good at telling my condensed version of the story, highlighting key points and leaving the rest for later conversations. Often the revelation would be followed by words of obligatory support from the listener, who would reassure me it was good that I had gotten out of those relationships.

But let's be honest. No one who learns that I have been married three times is ever going to be fully convinced that I've simply had a run of bad luck. It doesn't matter what valid explanations follow the revelation, it's absurd to think that anyone would walk away from our conversation with a good feeling about my overall emotional stability. The proverbial red flag is undeniable, flapping vigorously in the gusty winds of my excuses and rationalizations. They may not come out and say it, but people know something is not quite right. It doesn't mean my reasons for divorce weren't valid, or that anyone in my situation wouldn't also decide to end a marriage. But there was something deeper within my past that needed to be addressed ... something inside that was cycling me back to the same place of brokenness time and time again.

Why did I feel like I had to make excuses for myself?

The first reason was social.

Like it or not, just as we learned with the woman at the well, social status and marital status often go hand in hand. In the history of mankind, not much has changed. It's not the case everywhere you go, and it's not always intentional, but it is one of the ways social circles naturally form. Of course, we want to have friends and to make connections, and it can be difficult for a divorcee to fit in with a group of women who have single marriages and much more in common. Truth is, a strong marriage is at least a part of what brings a sense of pride, dignity and respectability to a woman amongst her peers.

The second reason for my need to explain was spiritual.

I sinned. I was constantly reminded that divorce is sin, and remarriage is sin. I made terrible mistakes *after* salvation, and continued to sin after I thought I had learned my lesson. It kept me tossing and turning at night, tearfully pleading with God for mercy, believing He was so angry with me the earth would open up beneath my bed and swallow me into hell—blanket, pillow, and all—with one furious, fiery bite. Sometimes I could not sleep; there was no rest in my spirit. I was depressed and afraid. Grace had undoubtedly been applied to my life, but I could not accept it because I had been raised to bear the burden of salvation by works, and I was failing miserably at it.

Some churches don't really know what to do with someone like me. For starters, many Christians are not in full agreement on when divorce is biblically permitted, and when it's not. A pastor won't suggest divorce in an abusive situation, but he also can't tell you in good conscience to stay in that marriage and inside the home (although some preachers will tell a woman to do precisely that), because the consequences can be physically or psychologically detrimental for you and your children. They may or may not call your salvation into question.

At the time I needed brothers and sisters in Christ to love and support me, I had come to one unsettling truth ... the social pariahs, vagrants, addicts, and reprobates would more readily embrace me and never lay judgment for what I had been through. In fact, the unsaved of this world were more likely to provide a feeling of acceptance without hesitation, without qualification, and without any sort of critical examination. The downcast and outcast would open their arms to me in a way many Christians would not and had not. I could walk into a small-town bar and claim more friends than inside a church building.

Those within the church failed me, and have failed countless brothers and sisters in Christ who desperately needed help during one of the lowest points in their lives. Had it not been for God and the mustard seed of genuine faith I had left, I would not be the overcomer I am today. I'll be boldly honest with you in saying I give little credit to the fellowship of believers during my time of suffering and healing. I was instead harassed and judged. It was just God and me for a long time. It took years of reading the Bible cover to cover, lying flat on the floor with my face in the carpet, crying and pleading with God for answers, to finally come to a place of peace within my spirit. For any child of God to be alone in their pain is not what Christ intended for His beloved Church. Generally speaking, when it comes to those suffering from the pain of divorce, many believers have fallen far short and have not been in alignment with the heart of Christ, and it needs to change.

Jesus healed the afflicted on the Sabbath, He ate with prostitutes and tax collectors, and kept an adulterous woman from a legal stoning. Jesus went out of His way to meet and talk to the Samaritan woman, who had been married five times, someone no one else wanted to associate with. These are examples of all His gracious acts which were not in keeping with the law or the religious and social practices of that day, and the Pharisees despised Him for it. They were following the letter of the law, much of which was added legalism, but Jesus was busy reaching hearts, healing, redeeming, and loving.

I know, I know. Jesus is the Physician for the spiritually sick, the *unsaved*. He was calling them to faith. I know what you're thinking ... it's different for believers in the fellowship, right? We are held to a higher standard. That is absolutely correct. But if the woman at the well had left that day and married even once more, would Jesus have taken back the 'living water' He offered her?

There is a lot of pain behind divorce. Much of the time, it goes all the way back to childhood, even infancy ... physical abuse, sexual abuse, distrust, trauma, and abandonment. Children are subjected to addiction, sexual immorality, anger, and violence with a parent or caregiver. Not many people have an opportunity to work through these issues before they marry the first time. They don't ever imagine that by young adulthood, their early life experiences will begin to affect their relationships moving forward. All they are able to see is how they can do things differently and make it better for themselves. Though well intentioned, they have misconceptions, and they don't understand what's lurking in the dark recesses of their psyche and how it will impact their lives.

Spiritual leaders often speak on their own authority and interpret scripture with limited understanding. In our Christian walk, what we speak, how we behave, and how we assess or discern the trials and tribulations of our brothers and sisters in Christ is an indication of the manner in which we are judging—either righteously and with loving discernment *or* with self-righteous pride and indignation. Are we speaking and behaving on our own authority? Or are we truly a reflection of Jesus toward those we are supposed to love to a greater extent than we love ourselves? Oftentimes, the law and consequences are callously pushed without a heart to listen, encourage, or aid in restoration.

When Jesus showed healing power on the Sabbath, was it more important that someone He loved was restored to health, or that the Pharisee's perception of God's strict guidelines be adhered to? Jesus said, *"If a man receives circumcision on the Sabbath so that the Law of Moses will not be broken, are you angry with Me because I made an entire man well on the Sabbath? Do not judge by the outward appearance, but judge with righteous judgment."* - John 7:23-24 (NASB1995)

Why do many Christians see divorce so much differently than they do any other sin? Why are we treating divorce like a terminal, incurable disease? Why do many in the Church believe a woman is legally and morally released from a spouse who abandons them, but a woman who's being beaten is not permitted the same peace? Just like the man Jesus healed on the Sabbath, in violation of the Law of Moses ... *What is more important*? It is a misunderstanding of Scripture and a total misrepresentation of the heart of God for anyone to think God would apply grace to abandonment, but not violence. Truth be told, I would rather remain legally married to someone who had abandoned me than to remain in the same home with someone who was physically or sexually abusive. I would rather be left high and dry than to cohabitate with someone who caused me to fear for my safety, or the well-being of my innocent children.

"But as for you, why do you judge your brother or sister? Or you as well, why do you regard your brother or sister with contempt? For we will all appear before the judgment seat of God. For it is written: 'As I live, says the Lord, To Me every knee will bow, And every tongue will give praise to God.' So then each one of us will give an account of himself to God. Therefore let's not judge one another anymore, but rather determine this: not to put an obstacle or a stumbling block in a brother's way." - Romans 14:10-13 (NASB1995)

Paul's intent was to encourage believers to use righteous discernment to help their brothers and sisters in Christ, and not to pass the wrong kind of judgment. There is a balance between counseling someone with biblical truth, in the spirit of love, and throwing a stumbling block in their path with pompous drivel, giving them the wrong idea of what our life in Christ is *not*.

Then in Romans 15:1-6 (NASB1995), *"Now we who are strong ought to bear the weaknesses of those without strength, and not just please ourselves. Each of us is to please his neighbor for his good, to his edification. For even Christ did not please Himself; but as it is written: 'The taunts of those who taunt You have fallen on Me.' For whatever was written in earlier times was written for our instruction, so that through perseverance and the encouragement of the Scriptures, we might have hope. Now may the God who gives perseverance and encouragement grant you to be of the same mind with one another, according to Christ Jesus, so that with one purpose and one voice you may glorify the God and Father of our Lord Jesus Christ."*

As it pertains to those who are counted among the brethren, Galatians 6:1 (NKJV) says, *"Brethren, if a man is overtaken in any trespass, you who are spiritual restore such a one in a spirit of gentleness, considering yourself lest you also be tempted. Bear one another's burdens, and so fulfill the law of Christ."*

The Bible is clear as to what the Church is instructed to do with those who have been "overtaken in a sin" or struggling in some way on a spiritual level. In Galatians 6:1, we are instructed to restore our brother or sister in a spirit of gentleness. We do this by bearing their burden, praying with and for them, being present, holding them accountable in a spirit of meekness, and sharing scripture to encourage them in the faith. Restoration does not happen with self-righteous criticism or angry rebuke. There is a time and place for a Jesus-style whip cracking and table turning, but this is not it.

In Matthew 7:1-5 (NASB1995) Jesus said, *"Do not judge, so that you will not be judged. For in the way you judge, you will be judged; and by your standard of measure, it will be measured to you. Why do you look at the speck that is in your brother's eye, but do not notice the log that is in your own eye? Or how can you say to your brother, 'Let me take the speck out of your eye,' and behold, the log is in your own eye? You hypocrite, first take the log out of your own eye, and then you will see clearly to take the speck out of your brother's eye!"*

At the time of my first divorce, I found a piece of paper taped to the steering wheel of my car, reminding me of scripture (used out of context) which states adulterers, among other sinners, will not inherit the kingdom of heaven (1 Corinthians 6:9-11). Others would warn me it would be better, spiritually, if I were to remain separated forever rather than divorce my spouse. I found a letter of rebuke in my mailbox from members of my church, and my father took every opportunity to warn me of the consequences. My grandfather told me no good man in his right mind would want to marry a divorced woman with children, so why would I divorce my kids' father? I became afraid to answer my door or my phone. It didn't matter the reason I had filed for divorce. They didn't want to listen; they didn't care about healing. All they could see was the law. In their minds, my salvation was on the line. My kids would not turn out right. My life would never be blessed.

There is a much deeper problem. If Christians would be less judgmental and give more time to prayerfully discerning a situation with godly wisdom, people who are hurting might actually recover and find peace. But this cannot be done without love and humility! If you don't have genuine love and concern for your brother or sister in Christ, you should not be extending yourself to "help" until *your* heart is in the right place, because a heart full of self-righteous pride will never understand their pain.

I do not write so that we feel at ease with willful sin and disobedience. I have made it clear, throughout this book, that marriage is a sacred covenant before God and not to be taken lightly. However, I write to advocate for those who are truly hurting or struggling, and who are living their lives in emotional and spiritual isolation. I'm writing to help those who truly love God and want healing that will result in better decisions.

I am taking a stand for those who wrongly believe God's grace cannot be applied to their situation.

Maybe you can identify with my story and have experienced judgmental or condemning words by church members. Maybe you are a deacon, pastor, the spouse, Sunday School teacher, or simply a man or woman of God who has devoted themselves to their local fellowship, but have failed in the past to see this as an important ministry within the church. Maybe you have even abused or misused your position in leadership by bringing undue fear to the hearts of believers.

Whatever the case, and from whichever end of the scope you are reading, I hope we can all learn from scripture what God expects of us as it relates to our brothers and sisters in Christ. If you are hurting, remember just because someone is a leader or well-respected member of the church doesn't mean they are correct in the way they are communicating with you. It's my goal to help you understand who God is, and how He sees your circumstances, no matter how bad it's become for you.

REFLECTIONS

Read John 7:10-24. Have you had an experience with other Christians or church leadership regarding a judgment that was made on appearance or without righteous judgment? Explain.

_____

_____

_____

_____

_____

Now, discuss and/or write about how proper biblical understanding could have changed the approach and outcome of the situation.

_____

_____

_____

_____

_____

Read 1 Corinthians chapter 5. How might an impending divorce between a married couple in your church require a different approach than someone, like the man in 1 Corinthians chapter 5, who is hardened and willful in their sin? How are they different?

_____

_____

_____

_____

_____

_____

_____

Prayer: *Jesus, please help us grow together, as brothers and sisters. Help me, as I move forward, to speak the truth in love, so that I can minister help and not hurt. Develop in me the compassion I need to pray for others in situations I may not always understand. Give me the wisdom to know when, if, and what I should speak, so that I can be a vessel of restoration rather than rebuked.*

CHAPTER NINE:

Moving Forward

1 Corinthians 7:27-28, Psalm 22, 1 Peter 2:21-25, 2 Corinthians 5:21, Isaiah 40:31

"*A re you bound to a wife? Do not seek to be released. Are you released from a wife? Do not seek a wife. But if you marry, you have not sinned; and if a virgin marries, she has not sinned. Yet such people will have trouble in this life, and I am trying to spare you.*" - 2 Timothy 1:12 Corinthians 7:27-28 (NASB1995)

Whether you are a man with a wife, or a wife with a husband, do not seek to be free from your spouse. If you are unmarried, do not seek to be bound. The general directive given by Paul is that neither the married nor the unmarried should *look for* a change in their marital status. This advice was given due to "present distress" happening at that time (likely persecution, indicated in verse 26), so singleness is not Paul's directive for all unmarried men (or women), for all time.

However, there are appropriate times to consider the benefits of an unconstrained, less complicated state of singleness. Remaining as you are may be a good idea for a number of reasons—peace, personal spiritual growth, or the current state of your mind and emotions, just to name a few. Haven't you had enough "trouble in the flesh" for a while?

Whether we move forward as a married or unmarried person, there are two things we all need to stop doing.

STOP LEAVING GOD OUT OF THE EQUATION

We have the ultimate source for healing, peace, and wholeness in the heavenly Father. Yet while we are chasing everything (and everyone) we think will make us happy, God is often ignored. We mess up again, then try to recover on our own, or we employ the help of other human beings ... and God is still ignored. We repeat the cycle, and fail to obey; we continue to struggle, and rarely find the time for prayer and worship.

Maybe you attend church every Sunday. Maybe you put money in the offering plate, teach Sunday School, or sing in the choir. You can do all of this and not be any closer to God. It's kind of like a husband telling his wife he needs more quality time with her, and she tells him, "What do you mean? I wash your laundry, I cook your meals, and I clean the toilets!" These dutiful acts are not enough if you want a beautiful and intimate relationship with your spouse, and it's not enough in a relationship with God.

"Oh, taste and see that the Lord is good; Blessed is the man who trusts in Him!" - Psalm 34:8 (NASB1995)

After my third divorce in March 2022, I had recovered from a 6-month illness. In 2023, I lost my father. I spent the next year taking care of my mother, who fell ill a few weeks after his death. I was also experiencing the depression that comes with empty nest syndrome, and was alone most of the time. Anxiety became an issue. I felt attacked by the enemy on all sides. I was hurt, grieving, and emotionally and physically drained from all of it.

One evening, it had gotten so bad that I had packed a suitcase. My intention was to take off without telling anyone where I was going. I didn't even know where I was going. I just wanted to drive off into the sunset, as if changing my geographical location would leave my problems in the dust the moment my car pulled out of the driveway.

My daughter became concerned and drove to my house. She sat with me as I cried over the events of the last few years. Everything had come to a head that night; I felt deep loss, hopelessness, and a lack of direction. I eventually fell asleep. When I woke the next morning to the same reality, I cried again. I could not bear any more loss or pain.

It helped that my daughter was with me, but the only thing that was able to pull my spirit out of despair was worship. I played some worship music over my sound system and I began to praise. I wasn't praying about my situation, or how I felt. I wasn't asking God for anything. I simply worshiped Him and began to focus on having a heart of gratitude. There was so much comfort in it. My spirit began to shift almost immediately. It moved me to search for blessings in the muck of my heartbreak. I pushed aside the mourning, the hurt, and every negative thing that was keeping me down, and I thanked Him for what He had done for me throughout my life.

"How marvelous You are, Oh Lord! How great are Your works! Thank You for Your kindness. Thank You for Your salvation. Thank You for my children. Thank You for protecting us...."

Psalm 22 is a prophetic psalm of David presenting Jesus Christ as the Savior who laid down His life for the sins of mankind. It was both a cry of anguish and a song of praise. The psalm begins by portraying the rejection and abandonment Christ suffered on the Cross. Jesus would speak these words from the Cross...

My God, My God, why have You forsaken Me?

Why are You so far from helping Me,

And from the words of My groaning?- Psalm 22:1-2 (NKJV)

Can you relate? Where are you, God? Where is the end of this distress? I cry out in the day, I cry out at night, and yet you do not answer me.

Psalm 22:1-2 is a prophetic picture of Jesus' anguish. However, in the next verse... *"But You are holy, Enthroned in the praises of Israel."* - Psalm 22:3 (NKJV)

In this beautiful, prophetic writing, Jesus, who was in tremendous suffering, declared His absolute trust in God by saying, "But You are holy, and You inhabit the praises of Israel." Because He chose to bear the punishment of the sins of humanity, Jesus Christ experienced pain and anguish on a level which has never been and can never be experienced by anyone in any situation.

Yet God was silent.

Jesus was suffering, and God did not answer.

"My God, my God! Why have You forsaken me?" God was seemingly absent in the time of absolute need. But Jesus reminded Himself of God's sovereignty.

"You inhabit the praises of your people."

The word "inhabit" gives us a picture of sitting, dwelling, or remaining somewhere. God dwells in your praise. He lives in your worship. That is where you will find Him!

Jesus was expressing His absolute trust in the heavenly Father even in His suffering. No matter what was happening, how bad it was, or how alone He felt, Jesus knew the Father was present in spite of His feelings. God was in control in His greatest hour of need. God had not abandoned Him. God had a plan.

So it is with God's children. When life bears down on you, when you can't see a way out, when you feel rejected... whatever your circumstance, draw close to Him, and He will draw close to you. Keep Him close. Stop pushing Him aside. Make your relationship with the Lord a daily priority. When you wake in the morning, worship the Lord. Come to Him first! He is our source! Your worship and gratitude is where you will find Him; the Lord dwells in your praise!

STOP THINKING YOU ARE NOT A PART OF THE PROBLEM

We are human beings and, therefore, a part of the problem. That doesn't mean you are necessarily responsible for your divorce, but it does mean that you are as inflicted with the human condition as the next person. You have made your own poor decisions, you have failed God and made mistakes in your relationships with your parents, spouse(s), friends, children, and co-workers, and in your interactions with perfect strangers.

Even the most peace-loving among us have their unsavory moments. Perhaps when someone hurts you, you come out "swinging," physically or verbally. The offense causes you to behave or speak in accordance with the flesh. At times, it's difficult to communicate to others as Jesus desires, and maybe you often choose to add fuel to the fire with your responses. Or, like me, you have a tendency to "run," emotionally. You find it difficult to trust and attach, which can deprive your spouse of his or her most basic needs, that is, a real connection outside of the bedroom. Whatever the case, even when the craziness is over, anger and resentment can build. What's worse, when the issues have not been addressed, you will most assuredly move on to the next relationship in that spirit, because it's too easy to point all of the blame on the spouse who may have been demonstrably more destructive.

"For you have been called for this purpose, because Christ also suffered for you, leaving you an example, so that you would follow in His steps: "He who committed no sin, Nor was any deceit found in His mouth"; and while being abusively insulted, He did not insult in return; while suffering, He did not threaten, but kept entrusting Himself to Him who judges righteously; and He Himself brought our sins in His body up on the cross, so that we might die to sin and live for righteousness; by His wounds you were healed. For you were continually straying like sheep, but now you have returned to the Shepherd and Guardian of your souls." - 1 Peter 2:21-25 (NASB1995)

Jesus is our example. He suffered for us so that we would follow in His steps. He committed no s n, nor was there any deceit found in Him. While being abusively insulted, He did not insult in return. Even while suffering, He did not threaten, but continued to entrust Himself to God.

How many of us can say the same?

Often, our solution to relationship problems is simply finding another imperfect human being, with different dysfunctions, in hopes that person will not hurt us the way the last relationship did. Maybe there has never been a time of serious introspection; nevertheless, there is work that must be done in all of us. To be clear, you are *not* the reason someone abused or mistreated you. You are not responsible for someone else's adultery, addiction, or general bad behavior. But it all has to be addressed, between you and God, for real change.

"He made Him who knew no sin to be sin on our behalf, so that we might become the righteousness of God in Him." - 2 Corinthians 5:21 (NASB1995)

Jesus suffered and died on the Cross not only to redeem you, but also to *change* you.

Jesus came to my well, my heart, the place of my brokenness. He didn't come to grant me popularity; He didn't bring me new friends. He didn't provide me with answers as to why I lost my mother, why I can't seem to make connections, or why I struggle in relationships. He didn't come to the well to give me a husband who would love me unconditionally, forever. He came to give me grace, peace, and a new purpose. He wasn't there to condemn me, but to establish my value and to give me genuine love and forgiveness, just as He did the woman at the well in John chapter four.

After that day with my daughter, I unpacked my suitcase and decided to change my focus by placing God at the head of my life in every way, including any potential romantic relationship, and fully pursue what I felt he had called me to do. Even in the midst of suffering, many wonderful things have happened as I have set aside the emptiness of human validation and chased after God. I had to admit that I was a part of my problems. My mindset got in the way. Disobedience hindered my prayers. When that changed, I changed for the better.

The spiritual captivity I felt from those around me was never the reality of my relationship with God. Just like the woman at the well, I believed something oppressive, something that kept me in bondage for many years, and I allowed it to get in the way of God's will for my life. Through trials and tribulations, and all my sin, Jesus never failed me. He loves me. He was—and is—always with me. Since the day I gave Him my heart as a little girl, He has kept me in His gracious and loving care. The same is true for you.

I was a bluebird perched peacefully on His finger. At last, there was no fear. I felt the gentle winds of freedom stir beneath my wings. He smiled and assured me that I am loved, I am capable, and that I would be okay. I was called to do greater things for His glory—it was time to spread my wings and fly.

"But those who wait on the Lord shall renew their strength; they shall mount up with wings like eagles, they shall run and not be weary, they shall walk and not faint." - Isaiah 40:31 (NKJV)

"For this reason I also suffer these things, but I am not ashamed; for I know whom I have believed, and I am convinced that He is able to protect what I have entrusted to Him until that day." - 2 Timothy 1:12 (NASB 1995)

REFLECTIONS

Discuss or Journal

As a practice of gratitude and worship, I want to thank God for...

_____
_____
_____
_____
_____

Read Isaiah 53:4-6. According to verse 6, who has gone astray?

_____
_____
_____
_____
_____

In what ways have you gone astray?

_____
_____
_____
_____

What can you do to change your responses, to God and to others?

_____
_____
_____

_____

_____
_____
_____

Write a *PRAYER* and *RESOLUTION* between you and God:

_____
_____
_____
_____
_____
_____
_____
_____
_____

Prayer: *Dear Heavenly Father, even in my distress I know that You are with me, and that You have a plan for my life. I am so grateful that You are attentive even in my hour of need. Help me to search my heart in an honest way, so that I can lay aside the sin that is not pleasing to You. In Jesus' name, Amen.*

www.ingramcontent.com/pod-product-compliance
Lightning Source LLC
Chambersburg PA
CBHW031434120626
46545CB00006B/2395